Modern Times, Epistles & Revelation

A Family Study Handbook

Combining all your students (grades 1–12)
for History, Geography, and Bible

by
Sonya Shafer

Modern Times, Epistles & Revelation: A Family Study Handbook
© 2012, Sonya Shafer

Cover Design: Ruth Shafer

ISBN 978-1-61634-173-2 printed
ISBN 978-1-61634-174-9 electronic download

Published by
Simply Charlotte Mason, LLC
P.O. Box 892
Grayson, Georgia 30017-0892

SimplyCharlotteMason.com

Contents

Introduction

I love to teach Bible history along with world events, and the first three handbooks in this series focus on Bible history from Genesis through Acts. Some time is spent studying world events that happened during those years, but the emphasis is on Biblical history.

With the fourth handbook, the focus changes a little. We no longer have Biblical events to study, and world history picks up the pace. So with the fourth, fifth, and sixth books, we delve into learning about people who lived in the past since the time of the book of Acts, and we combine that study with timeless truths from the Epistles. This sixth book focuses on Modern history, about 1850 to the present.

The lessons in this book will walk you through living books to read, Scripture passages to study, and optional hands-on activities to do. You'll also find narration ideas, teaching tips, exam questions, and Book of Centuries dates.

One of my main goals is to show you how you can teach the same historical time period to all of your children at the same time, no matter what grades they are in. I firmly believe in the advantages that a one-room schoolhouse approach can bring. You will save time in both planning and teaching, and your children will grow together in community as they learn together and help each other.

Please keep in mind that this study is just a collection of suggestions. I'm simply passing along these suggestions to, hopefully, save you some time and give you some ideas. You know your children much better than I do, so feel free to change, add, or omit as you see fit. Remember, I used the books that were available to me; they may not be available to you. Don't be afraid to substitute.

Most of all, encourage the older children to help the younger, and allow the younger to look over the shoulder of the older; and together, enjoy these family studies of History, Geography, and God's Word.

How to Use

Pace

The lessons are divided into three Terms. If you do five lessons each week, you should be able to cover a Term in about twelve weeks. Each week is divided into two days of American History, one day of Geography and Bible, and two days of World History. With this format you should be able to easily substitute your own country's history if you are not American. We have tried to save the final week of each Term for exams or to finish up any projects or assignments.

The chart below gives an overview of what is covered each Term. You will find more detailed charts, outlining work week by week, at the beginning of the Terms' lesson plans.

	American History (2 days/week)	Geography & Bible (1 day/week)	World History (2 days/week)
Term 1	Oregon Trail through Theodore Roosevelt	North America & 1 Peter, 2 Peter, Jude, 1 John	Bismarck through George Mueller
Term 2	Wright Brothers through end of World War II	United States & 1 John, 2 John, 3 John, Revelation	Boer War through end of World War II
Term 3	Cold War through present day	United States & Revelation	Creation of Israel through present day

Assignments

This book contains assignments and activities for every grade level so you can combine all your students into one family study. The "Family" instructions are for everyone to do together, then additional assignments are given for various grade levels to complete either independently or with the parent.

The hands-on activities are optional. Feel free to skip them, substitute different ones, or add more. You will find lots of helpful information and Internet links on the Links and Tips page for this book on our Web site at http://SimplyCharlotteMason.com/books/modern/links-tips

Note: Don't worry about days when you might skip the lesson for younger children but still do a lesson with the older children. Think of it as a day that the younger children can ruminate on what they have already learned. Charlotte encouraged reflecting, or ruminating, on what is read or heard: ". . . Reflection, the ruminating power which is so strongly developed in children and is somehow lost with much besides of the precious cargo they bring with them into the world. There is nothing sadder than the way we allow intellectual impressions to pass over the surface of our minds, without any effort to retain or assimilate" (Vol. 3, p. 120). "Children must be allowed to ruminate, must be left alone with their own thoughts" (Vol. 3, p. 162).

Resources Needed

A complete list of resources is given on pages 15–17 for all three Terms. Each Term's resources are listed in the lesson plans. Reminders are sprinkled throughout the lessons that will help you look ahead a week or so in order to give yourself enough time to locate the books you will need, especially if you are borrowing them as you go.

Map Drill

One part of most Geography lessons will be a map drill. Here's how we do map drill. Keep lessons short, no longer than ten or fifteen minutes. Once a week, give each child a blank map of the region you are studying and provide a detailed and labeled map of the same region. Instruct the child to label a few areas of the region, being careful to copy the names correctly from the detailed map. The next week, give the child another blank map of the same region and instruct her to label as many areas as she can remember. Once she has labeled all that she knows, display the detailed map and check for accuracy, then have her label a few more areas carefully. Continue this routine each week, and over the course of the year she will become quite familiar with the regions studied using this gentle method.

www.SimplyCharlotteMason.com

A Word about Charlotte Mason Methods Used in This Study

Living Books

Probably the most well known of Charlotte Mason's methods is her use of living books instead of dry, factual textbooks. Living books are usually written by one person who has a passion for the subject and writes in conversational or narrative style. The books pull you into the subject and involve your emotions, so it's easy to remember the events and facts. Living books make the subject "come alive." The books used in this study are living books. If you make a substitution, please do your best to select a living book.

Bible Readings

The Bible is the best living book! And Charlotte encouraged us to give our children plenty of direct contact with the Bible itself, not feed them just watered down retellings. So you will find throughout the lessons, the Scripture passages to read aloud directly from the Bible.

Narration

When you ask a child to narrate, you're asking him to tell back in his own words what he just saw, heard, or read. The narration can be oral or written or drawn— whatever. Because the child must think through the information and determine how to present it, mixed with his own opinion and impressions, this method of evaluation requires a much higher thinking level than mere fill-in-the-blank or answer-the-posed-question-with-a-fact methods. When requesting a child to narrate, word the question in an open, essay-type form, such as "Tell all you know about ___" or "Describe ___."

Oral Narration with Many Children: Usually it's good to start with the youngest child, then work your way up the ages asking if each has anything to add. However, if you use this approach every single time, the older ones might get complacent. ("No, nothing to add.") So you can mix things up a little by calling on any child at random to start the narration sometimes. Not knowing who will be selected to give the oral narration keeps everybody alert and listening. The key is to have one child start the narration and then have the others add to it, not repeat it. That mental exercise of remembering what was already mentioned and searching through your mind for something new to talk about is also a plus!

Written Narration: Older children can be expected to take the next step and write their narrations. If your older child is not used to doing narration, give him several weeks or months to get used to the idea and have practice narrating orally first. It's harder to keep your train of thought when you have to also think about the mechanics of writing, punctuating, capitalizing, and all such trappings, so make sure your child is adept and successful with organizing and expressing his thoughts orally before adding the writing aspect. Once he is an "old pro" at oral narrations, you can ease him into the written narrations by requiring just one a week or so to begin with. The lessons in this book will give suggestions for some written narrations. You can determine which of your students can handle those assignments.

Also keep in mind that you can do narration in many ways. Oral is the quickest and simplest. But if you would like to keep things fresh, you can have the children express what they learned in various ways. We have a list of narration ideas on the Web site that might help you: http://SimplyCharlotteMason.com/timesavers/narration/

Book of Centuries

A Book of Centuries is like a timeline in a notebook. As its name suggests, each two-page spread in the book is devoted to one hundred years—a century—of history. Each student creates his or her own book, recording historical events and names of importance, along with pictures, poems, quotes, and anything else that makes the book individual. You can also add written narrations, illustrations from the Internet, or titles of books you've read that are set in that time period. As they add more history to the book, they begin to make relations between people who lived in the same era.

Books of Centuries can be as simple or elaborate as you desire. If you want a simple one, download a free Book of Centuries template at SimplyCharlotteMason.com/timesavers/boc/

We recommend each student in grades 7–12 create his own Book of Centuries. If your students are not yet old enough to take on the responsibility of their own Books of Centuries, you could create one together as a family.

Watch for helpful dates in the timeline column throughout the lessons in this book. You don't have to add every event listed; feel free to pick and choose or add some of your own.

Resources Needed

American History

- *Stories of America, Volume 2*, by Charles Morris, et al.
  Though written for the younger grades, this gentle introduction to American history will make a nice Family spine, contribute some additional biographies and information, and help tie together the different characters the older students will be reading about.
- *Our Country's Presidents* by Ann Bausum (reference book)
- *The Story of Thomas A. Edison* by Frances M. Perry
- *The Brooklyn Bridge* by Elizabeth Mann
- ✓*Empire State Building* by Elizabeth Mann
- *Hoover Dam* by Elizabeth Mann
- *Billy Graham: God's Ambassador* by Russ Busby
  OR *Billy Graham: Just Get Up Out of Your Seat* by Catherine Mackenzie
  Both books on Billy Graham are good. *Billy Graham: God's Ambassador* reads like a scrapbook with numerous photographs and souvenirs from across the years that make Rev. Graham's life come alive. *Billy Graham: Just Get Up Out of Your Seat* reads more like a story.

Grades 1–3
- *Abraham Lincoln* by Ingri and Edgar d'Aulaire
- *Buffalo Bill* by Ingri and Edgar d'Aulaire
- *Sarah, Plain and Tall* by Patricia MacLachlan
- *A Boy Named FDR: How Franklin D. Roosevelt Grew Up to Change America* by Kathleen Krull
- *Franklin and Winston: A Christmas That Changed the World* by Douglas Wood
- *Rebekkah's Journey: A World War II Refugee Story* by Ann E. Burg
- *Lily's Victory Garden* by Helen L. Wilbur
- *The Unbreakable Code* by Sara Hoagland Hunter
- *I Have a Dream: The Story of Martin Luther King* by Margaret Davidson
- *Moonshot: The Flight of Apollo 11* by Brian Floca

Grades 4–6
- *Abe Lincoln: Log Cabin to White House* by Sterling North
- *Always Inventing: A Photobiography of Alexander Graham Bell* by Tom L. Matthews
- *The Wright Brothers: Pioneers of American Aviation* by Quentin Reynolds
- *I Have a Dream: The Story of Martin Luther King* by Margaret Davidson
- *Team Moon: How 400,000 People Landed Apollo 11 on the Moon* by Catherine Thimmesh
- *Our Country's Presidents* by Ann Bausum (reference book)

Grades 7–9
- *Lincoln: A Photobiography* by Russell Freedman
- *Across Five Aprils* by Irene Hunt
- *Bully for You, Teddy Roosevelt* by Jean Fritz
- *The Wright Brothers: How They Invented the Airplane* by Russell Freedman
- *The Yanks Are Coming* by Albert Marrin
- *Victory in the Pacific* by Albert Marrin
- *Roll of Thunder, Hear My Cry* by Mildred D. Taylor
- *Ronald Reagan: Destiny at His Side* by Janet and Geoff Benge
- Book of Centuries (one for each student)

Grades 10–12
- *Lincoln: A Photobiography* by Russell Freedman
- *The Red Badge of Courage* by Stephen Crane

- *American Voices: A Collection of Documents, Speeches, Essays, Hymns, Poems, and Short Stories from American History* edited by Ray Notgrass
  This collection is used over two years. Selections are assigned throughout the Early Modern handbook, that covers 1550 through 1850, and in this handbook.
- *Bully for You, Teddy Roosevelt* by Jean Fritz
- *The Wright Brothers: How They Invented the Airplane* by Russell Freedman
- *America: The Last Best Hope, Volume 2: From a World at War to the Triumph of Freedom* by William Bennett
- *The Yanks Are Coming* by Albert Marrin
- *Victory in the Pacific* by Albert Marrin
- *Freedom Walkers* by Russell Freedman
- *America: The Last Best Hope, Volume 3: From the Collapse of Communism to the Rise of Radical Islam* by William Bennett
- Book of Centuries (one for each student)

Note: We recommend that grades 10–12 students add an American Government course either during this Modern Times study or spread over two years, during Early Modern and Modern Times studies.

Optional Resources
- *George Washington Carver* by David Collins (grades 1–3)
  This biography on Carver is completely appropriate for younger children, but the chapters may be too long for some younger students in addition to the Family reading. Use your discretion whether to include it in your studies.
- *Up From Slavery* by Booker T. Washington (grades 7–12)
- *The Story of My Life* by Helen Keller (grades 7–12)
- Dover coloring books
  Dover offers so many history coloring books set in this time period that we cannot list them all here. Below is just a sampling of titles. Visit their website at http://DoverPublications.com for a full listing.
  Abraham Lincoln
  Airplanes of the Second World War
  American Presidents
  Antique Automobiles
  A Soldier's Life in the Civil War
  Story of the California Gold Rush
  Story of the Civil War
  Story of the Underground Railroad
  Teddy Roosevelt
  Western Pioneers
- Various resources for optional hands-on projects

World History, Bible, Geography Resources
- *Stories of the Nations, Volume 2*, by Lorene Lambert
  Though written for the younger grades, these gentle introductions to famous men of the time period will make a nice Family spine, contribute some additional biographies and information, and help tie together the different characters the older students will be reading about.
- *George Mueller* by Faith Coxe Bailey
- *Gandhi: The Young Protester Who Founded a Nation* by Philip Wilkinson
- *Mandela: The Rebel Who Led His Nation to Freedom* by Ann Kramer
- *GOAL Bible Study Journal* by Sonya Shafer
- *Come, Lord Jesus: A Revelation Bible Study* by Sonya Shafer

- Bible
- *The Tree in the Trail* and *Minn of the Mississippi* and *Paddle to the Sea* by Holling C. Holling

OR *WorldTrek* by Russell and Carla Fisher

   The Holling books are centered on American geography and history. If you want a book that is not centered in the U. S., read *WorldTrek*, which chronicles a family's self-guided trip around the world.
- *Uncle Josh's Outline Map book or CD* by George and Hannah Wiggers (or other outline maps of North America and the United States)
- Labeled world map
- Labeled United States map

Grades 1–3
- *Only a Dog: A Story of the Great War* by Bertha Whitridge Smith
- *The Little Ships: The Heroic Rescue at Dunkirk in World War II* by Louise Borden
- *Always Remember Me: How One Family Survived World War II* by Marisabina Russo
- *The Journey that Saved Curious George* by Louise Borden

Grades 4–6
- *Louis Pasteur: Founder of Modern Medicine* by John Hudson Tiner
- *The Singing Tree* by Kate Seredy
- *Where Poppies Grow: A World War I Companion* by Linda Granfield
- *Snow Treasure* by Marie McSwigan
- *Brother Andrew: God's Secret Agent* by Janet and Geoff Benge

Grades 7–9
- *Louis Pasteur: Founder of Modern Medicine* by John Hudson Tiner
- *Rescue and Redeem: Volume 5: Chronicles of the Modern Church* by Mindy and Brandon Withrow
- *Across America on an Emigrant Train* by Jim Murphy
- *World War I: From the Lusitania to Versailles* by Zachary Kent
- *The Endless Steppe* by Esther Hautzig
- *Animal Farm* by George Orwell
- *Swifter, Higher, Stronger: A Photographic History of the Summer Olympics* by Sue Macy
- *Discovering Doctrine* by Sonya Shafer (one for each student)
- Book of Centuries (one for each student)

   Note: As of the writing of this handbook, Famous Men of the 19th Century *and* Famous Men of the 20th Century *by Rob Shearer were not yet available from Greenleaf Press. When they are released, you could add them to the schedule.*

Grades 10–12
- *How Should We Then Live?* by Francis A Schaeffer

OR *7 Men Who Rule the World from the Grave* by Dave Breese

   Both suggested books are written from a Christian point of view. *How Should We Then Live?* is a review of world history from ancient Rome through the mid 1970s, examining the prominent worldviews based on writings, art, music, and society. It is a discussion about philosophy and its changes through the years. There is also a DVD series by the same name that covers the material.

   The alternate, *7 Men Who Rule the World from the Grave,* focuses on the twentieth century, discussing those men whom the author considers the progenitors of the most influential movements of that time and dealing with the way they have contended for our minds.
- *Rescue and Redeem: Volume 5: Chronicles of the Modern Church* by Mindy and Brandon Withrow
- *The War to End All Wars: World War I* by Russell Freedman
- *Hitler* by Albert Marrin
- *Stalin: Russia's Man of Steel* by Albert Marrin

- *Discovering Doctrine* by Sonya Shafer (one for each student)
- Book of Centuries (one for each student)

> Note: As of the writing of this handbook, Famous Men of the 19th Century *and* Famous Men of the 20th Century *by Rob Shearer were not yet available from Greenleaf Press. When they are released, you could add them to the schedule.*

Optional Resources
- *The Hiding Place* by Corrie Ten Boom (grades 10–12)
- Dover coloring books
  Dover history coloring books are also available for world history events for this time period. Here are a few titles. Check http://DoverPublications.com for a full listing.
  History of Flight
  International Space Station
  Victorian Fashions
  The Victorian House

**Visit our CM Bookfinder at http://apps.simplycharlottemason.com/
for more information on each book, including where to find it.**

Term 1
(12 weeks; 5 lessons/week)

American History Resources
- ✓ *Stories of America, Volume 2*, by Charles Morris, et al.
- • *Our Country's Presidents* by Ann Bausum (reference book)
- ✓ *The Story of Thomas A. Edison* by Frances M. Perry
- ✓ *The Brooklyn Bridge* by Elizabeth Mann

Grades 1–3
- ✓ *Abraham Lincoln* by Ingri and Edgar d'Aulaire
- ✓ *Buffalo Bill* by Ingri and Edgar d'Aulaire
- ✓ *Sarah, Plain and Tall* by Patricia MacLachlan

Grades 4–6
- ✓ *Abe Lincoln: Log Cabin to White House* by Sterling North
- ✓ *Always Inventing: A Photobiography of Alexander Graham Bell* by Tom L. Matthews

Grades 7–9
- • *Lincoln: A Photobiography* by Russell Freedman
- • *Across Five Aprils* by Irene Hunt
- • *Bully for You, Teddy Roosevelt* by Jean Fritz
- • Book of Centuries (one for each student)

Grades 10–12
- • *Lincoln: A Photobiography* by Russell Freedman
- • *The Red Badge of Courage* by Stephen Crane
- • *American Voices* edited by Ray Notgrass
- • *Bully for You, Teddy Roosevelt* by Jean Fritz
- • Book of Centuries (one for each student)

Optional Resources
- • Dover coloring books
- • Various resources for optional hands-on projects
- • *Up From Slavery* by Booker T. Washington (grades 7–12)
- • *The Story of My Life* by Helen Keller (grades 7–12)

World History, Bible, Geography Resources
- ✓ *Stories of the Nations, Volume 2*, by Lorene Lambert
- ✓ *George Mueller* by Faith Coxe Bailey
- • *GOAL Bible Study Journal* by Sonya Shafer
- • Bible
- ✓ *The Tree in the Trail* by Holling C. Holling
  OR *WorldTrek* by Russell and Carla Fisher
- • *Uncle Josh's Outline Map book or CD* by George and Hannah Wiggers (North America)
- • Labeled world map

Grades 1–3
(No additional reading this term)

Grades 4–6

✓ *Louis Pasteur: Founder of Modern Medicine* by John Hudson Tiner

✓ *The Singing Tree* by Kate Seredy

Grades 7–9

- *Louis Pasteur: Founder of Modern Medicine* by John Hudson Tiner
- *Rescue and Redeem: Volume 5: Chronicles of the Modern Church* by Mindy and Brandon Withrow
- *Discovering Doctrine* by Sonya Shafer (one for each student)
- Book of Centuries (one for each student)

Grades 10–12

- *How Should We Then Live?* by Francis A Schaeffer
  OR *7 Men Who Rule the World from the Grave* by Dave Breese
- *Rescue and Redeem: Volume 5: Chronicles of the Modern Church* by Mindy and Brandon Withrow
- *Discovering Doctrine* by Sonya Shafer (one for each student)
- Book of Centuries (one for each student)

Optional Resources

- Dover coloring books

	Family	Grades 1–3	4–6	7–9	10–12
Week 1, Lessons 1–5					
American History	Stories of America, Vol. 2, ch. 1, 2	Abraham Lincoln, parts A, B	Abe Lincoln: Log Cabin to White House, ch. 1, 2	Lincoln: A Photobiography, ch. 1–3	Lincoln: A Photobiography, ch. 1–3; American Voices, p. 176
Geography	Tree in the Trail, ch. 1–3, OR WorldTrek, pp. 11–16; Map Drill: North America				
Bible	1 Peter 1				
World History	Stories of the Nations, Vol. 2, ch. 1, 2		Louis Pasteur, ch. 1, 2	Louis Pasteur, ch. 1, 2	How Should We Then Live, ch. 1, OR 7 Men Who Rule the World, Introduction
Week 2, Lessons 6–10					
American History	Stories of America, Vol. 2, ch. 3, 4 and poem; Our Country's Presidents	Abraham Lincoln, parts C, D	Abe Lincoln: Log Cabin to White House, ch. 3, 4	Lincoln: A Photobiography, ch. 4, 5	Lincoln: A Photobiography, ch. 4, 5; American Voices, pp. 177–186, 193–197
Geography	Tree in the Trail, ch. 4, 5, OR WorldTrek, pp. 16–24; Map Drill: North America				
Bible	1 Peter 2				
World History	Stories of the Nations, Vol. 2, ch. 3, 4		Louis Pasteur, ch. 3, 4	Louis Pasteur, ch. 3, 4	How Should We Then Live, ch. 2, OR 7 Men Who Rule the World, ch. 1, 2
Week 3, Lessons 11–15					
American History	Stories of America, Vol. 2, ch. 5, 6	Buffalo Bill, pp. 1–20	Abe Lincoln: Log Cabin to White House, ch. 5, 6	Lincoln: A Photobiography, ch. 6, 7	Lincoln: A Photobiography, ch. 6, 7; American Voices, pp. 198–204, 212–215, 232–235
Geography	Tree in the Trail, ch. 6–8, OR WorldTrek, pp. 26–34; Map Drill: North America				
Bible	1 Peter 3				
World History	Stories of the Nations, Vol. 2, ch. 5; George Mueller, ch. 1		Louis Pasteur, ch. 5, 6	Louis Pasteur, ch. 5, 6	How Should We Then Live, ch. 3A, OR 7 Men Who Rule the World, ch. 3
Week 4, Lessons 16–20					
American History	Stories of America, Vol. 2, ch. 7, 8	Buffalo Bill, pp. 21–40	Abe Lincoln: Log Cabin to White House, ch. 7, 8	Across Five Aprils, ch. 1, 2	Red Badge of Courage, ch. 1–4; American Voices, pp. 236–240
Geography	Tree in the Trail, ch. 9, 10, OR WorldTrek, pp. 34–44; Map Drill: North America				
Bible	1 Peter 4				
World History	George Mueller, ch. 2, 3		Louis Pasteur, ch. 7, 8	Louis Pasteur, ch. 7, 8	How Should We Then Live, ch. 3B, OR 7 Men Who Rule the World, ch. 4A

Week 5, Lessons 21–25					
American History	Story of Thomas Edison, ch. 1–4		Abe Lincoln: Log Cabin to White House, ch. 9, 10A	Across Five Aprils, ch. 3, 4	Red Badge of Courage, ch. 5–8; American Voices, pp. 241–245
Geography	Tree in the Trail, ch. 11–13, OR WorldTrek, pp. 45–55; Map Drill: North America				
Bible	1 Peter 5				
World History	George Mueller, ch. 4, 5		Louis Pasteur, ch. 9, 10	Louis Pasteur, ch. 9, 10	How Should We Then Live, ch. 4, OR 7 Men Who Rule the World, ch. 4B, 5
Week 6, Lessons 26–30					
American History	Story of Thomas Edison, ch. 5–8		Abe Lincoln: Log Cabin to White House, ch. 10B, 11A	Across Five Aprils, ch. 5, 6	Red Badge of Courage, ch. 9–12; American Voices, pp. 247, 248
Geography	Tree in the Trail, ch. 14, 15, OR WorldTrek, pp. 55–59; Map Drill: North America				
Bible	2 Peter 1				
World History	George Mueller, ch. 6, 7		Louis Pasteur, ch. 11, 12	Louis Pasteur, ch. 11, 12	How Should We Then Live, ch. 5, OR 7 Men Who Rule the World, ch. 6A
Week 7, Lessons 31–35					
American History	Story of Thomas Edison, ch. 9–12	Sarah, Plain and Tall, ch. 1	Abe Lincoln: Log Cabin to White House, ch. 11B, 12	Across Five Aprils, ch. 7, 8	Red Badge of Courage, ch. 13–16; American Voices, pp. 249–252
Geography	Tree in the Trail, ch. 16–18, OR WorldTrek, pp. 59–62; Map Drill: North America				
Bible	2 Peter 2				
World History	George Mueller, ch. 8, 9		Louis Pasteur, ch. 13, 14	Louis Pasteur, ch. 13, 14	How Should We Then Live, ch. 6, OR 7 Men Who Rule the World, ch. 6B
Week 8, Lessons 36–40					
American History	Stories of America, Vol. 2, ch. 9, 10	Sarah, Plain and Tall, ch. 2, 3	Always Inventing, pp. 8–23	Across Five Aprils, ch. 9, 10	Red Badge of Courage, ch. 17–21; American Voices, pp. 253, 143–145
Geography	Tree in the Trail, ch. 19, 20, OR WorldTrek, pp. 63–70; Map Drill: North America				
Bible	2 Peter 3				
World History	George Mueller, ch. 10, 11		Louis Pasteur, ch. 15	Louis Pasteur, ch. 15; Rescue and Redeem, pp. 11–16	How Should We Then Live, ch. 7; Rescue and Redeem, pp. 11–16

Week 9, Lessons 41–45					
American History	Stories of America, Vol. 2, ch. 11, 12; poem; Our Country's Presidents	Sarah, Plain and Tall, ch. 4, 5	Always Inventing, pp. 24–37	Across Five Aprils, ch. 11, 12; Bully for You, Teddy Roosevelt, ch. 1	Red Badge of Courage, ch. 22–24; American Voices, pp. 275–277, 285–292; Bully for You, Teddy Roosevelt, ch. 1
Geography	Tree in the Trail, ch. 21–23, OR WorldTrek, pp. 70–79; Map Drill: North America				
Bible	Jude				
World History	George Mueller, ch. 12, 13		The Singing Tree, ch. 1	Rescue and Redeem, pp. 17–62	Rescue and Redeem, pp. 17–62
Week 10, Lessons 46–50					
American History	Stories of America, Vol. 2, ch. 13, 14	Sarah, Plain and Tall, ch. 6, 7	Always Inventing, pp. 38–57	Bully for You, Teddy Roosevelt, ch. 2, 3	Bully for You, Teddy Roosevelt, ch. 2, 3
Geography	Tree in the Trail, ch. 24, 25, OR WorldTrek, pp. 79–85; Map Drill: North America				
Bible	1 John 1				
World History	George Mueller, ch. 14, 15		The Singing Tree, ch. 2, 3	Rescue and Redeem, pp. 63–99	Rescue and Redeem, pp. 63–99
Week 11, Lessons 51–55					
American History	Stories of America, Vol. 2, ch. 15; Our Country's Presidents; The Brooklyn Bridge	Sarah, Plain and Tall, ch. 8, 9	Always Inventing, pp. 58–60	Bully for You, Teddy Roosevelt, ch. 4, 5	Bully for You, Teddy Roosevelt, ch. 4, 5; American Voices, p. 293
Geography	Tree in the Trail, ch. 26, 27, OR WorldTrek, pp. 86–92; Map Drill: North America				
Bible	1 John 2				
World History	George Mueller, ch. 16, 17		The Singing Tree, ch. 4, 5	Rescue and Redeem, pp. 101–147	Rescue and Redeem, pp. 101–147
Week 12, Lessons 56–60					
American History	Exam or Project			Bully for You, Teddy Roosevelt, ch. 6, 7	Bully for You, Teddy Roosevelt, ch. 6, 7
Geography	Exam				
Bible	Exam				
World History	Exam				

Lesson 1: Heading West on the Oregon Trail

Materials Needed
- *Stories of America, Vol. 2*
- *Abraham Lincoln* (grades 1–3)
- *Abe Lincoln: Log Cabin to White House* (grades 4–6)
- *Lincoln: A Photobiography* (grades 7–12)
- *American Voices* (grades 10–12)

Family: Ask students what they remember about how America grew from just thirteen colonies crowded against the Atlantic Ocean. Explain that as America grew in land, we needed people to go live on that land and settle it. Read together *Stories of America, Volume 2*, chapter 1, "Heading West on the Oregon Trail," and ask for an oral narration. Use the map on page 237 of *Stories of America, Volume 2*, as described in the chapter.

Settlers head west on the Oregon Trail (1843–1869)

Grades 1–3: Remind students that not everyone went as far west as Oregon; some Americans settled the land in between too. Begin reading with your younger children *Abraham Lincoln*. This book has no page numbers. For today's reading, go from the beginning ("Deep in the wilderness . . .") through their building the three-sided shelter (". . . they plowed and planted between the tree stumps."). Ask for an oral narration.

Grades 4–6: Read with your older children or assign as independent reading *Abe Lincoln: Log Cabin to White House,* chapter 1, "Nancy's Boy Baby." Ask for an oral or written narration.

Grades 7–12: Read with your older children or assign as independent reading *Lincoln: A Photobiography,* chapters 1 and 2, "The Mysterious Mr. Lincoln" and "A Backwoods Boy." Ask for an oral or written narration.

Grades 10–12: Also read with your older children or assign as independent reading *American Voices*, page 176, poems by Emily Dickinson.

Tip: Your older students will read many poems and hymn lyrics as they progress through American Voices. *Those selections make an interesting informal study of literary expectations and religious expression as they have changed over the years.*

Lesson 2: The California Gold Rush

Materials Needed
- *Stories of America, Vol. 2*
- *Abraham Lincoln* (grades 1–3)
- *Abe Lincoln: Log Cabin to White House* (grades 4–6)
- *Lincoln: A Photobiography* (grades 7–12)

**Book of Centuries
Timeline**

*Miners rush to California to dig for
gold (1848–1859)*

Family: Ask students what they remember about people traveling to the West Coast on the Oregon Trail. Explain that something happened on that coast that made many people want to get there quickly. Read together *Stories of America, Volume 2*, chapter 2, "The California Gold Rush," and ask for an oral narration.

Grades 1–3: Ask students what they recall about Abraham Lincoln as a child and the family's move to Little Pigeon Creek. Continue reading with your younger children *Abraham Lincoln*, from where you left off ("That winter was long . . .") through Abe's fight with the pirates (". . . he had a white scar over his eyebrow."). Ask for an oral narration.

Grades 4–6: Read with your older children or assign as independent reading *Abe Lincoln: Log Cabin to White House,* chapter 2, "The Half-Face Camp." Ask for an oral or written narration.

Grades 7–12: Read with your older children or assign as independent reading *Lincoln: A Photobiography,* chapter 3, "Law and Politics." Ask for an oral or written narration.

Reminder: Get the book Buffalo Bill *for grades 1–3 for lesson 11.*

Lesson 3: Geography Book and 1 Peter 1

Materials Needed
- *The Tree in the Trail* OR *WorldTrek*
- Outline map of North America; labeled world map
- Bible
- *GOAL Bible Study Journal*
- *Discovering Doctrine* (grades 7–12)

Family Geography Book: Read together *The Tree in the Trail*, chapters 1–3, and ask for an oral narration. Be sure to look often at the map in the back of the book to see the tree's location and how it relates to the other events you will read about.

If you would prefer a geography book not centered in the United States, read together *WorldTrek*, pages 11–16, and trace the Fishers' route on a world map or globe.

Family Map Drill: Give each student a copy of a blank outline map of North America. Encourage them to label all the countries that they know on the map. Most North America maps focus on Mexico, United States, and Canada. If you are using the map from *Uncle Josh's Outline Map Book*, students will have an opportunity to also review the countries of Central America plus the islands off the coast and Greenland (an autonomous country within the Kingdom of Denmark). Compare their labeled countries with a labeled world map and make any necessary corrections. Then have them label two or three more countries on their maps, copying the spelling and locations from the labeled world map.

Tip: Once a student knows those countries listed above, he can start working on learning the Canadian provinces. We will add the U. S. states in Terms 2 and 3.

Family Bible Study: Read together 1 Peter 1, looking for any descriptions of promises, commands, sins, or principles, as explained in your *GOAL Bible Study Journal*:

Grasp this promise.
Obey this command.
Avoid this sin.
Live this principle.
    Record your findings in your *GOAL Bible Study Journal*.

Tip: Older students should also be listening for doctrinal truths that they can add to their ongoing Discovering Doctrine *books.*

Tip: Be sure to review your GOAL findings each day of the week in order to help keep them in the forefront of everyone's minds. You won't see reminders in every lesson in this book, so set a time now that will work best for a quick read-through each day.

Tip: If you would like to download a free bookmark that will remind you of the GOAL items to look for in a passage, visit http://simplycharlottemason.com/books/goal-bible-study-journal/links-tips/ You might want to print a bookmark for each child, so they can refer to them during your family Bible study times.

 # Lesson 4: The Modern World

Materials Needed
- *Stories of the Nations, Vol. 2*
- *Louis Pasteur* (grades 4–9)
- *How Should We Then Live?* OR *7 Men Who Rule the World from the Grave* (grades 10–12)

Family: Ask students what they think the word "modern" means. Discuss how it could seem to change in meaning over the years, based on the time in which you are living. Read together *Stories of the Nations, Volume 2*, chapter 1, "The Modern World." Ask for an oral narration.

Grades 4–9: Read with your older children or assign as independent

Book of Centuries Timeline

Louis Pasteur proves germ theory; develops rabies vaccination and pasteurization (1822–1895)

reading *Louis Pasteur*, chapter 1, "City of a Thousand Dreams." Ask for an oral or written narration.

Grades 10–12: Read with your older children or assign as independent reading *How Should We Then Live?*, chapter 1, "Ancient Rome," OR the Introduction of *7 Men Who Rule the World from the Grave*. Ask for an oral or written narration.

Tip: Both suggested books are written from a Christian point of view. How Should We Then Live? *is a review of world history from ancient Rome through the mid 1970s, examining the prominent worldviews based on writings, art, music, and society. It is a discussion about philosophy and its changes through the years. There is also a DVD series by the same name that covers the material.*
The alternate, 7 Men Who Rule the World from the Grave, *focuses on the twentieth century, discussing those men whom the author considers the progenitors of the most influential movements of that time and dealing with the way they have contended for our minds.*

Lesson 5: How Bismarck Made an Empire

Materials Needed
- *Stories of the Nations, Vol. 2*
- *Louis Pasteur* (grades 4–9)

Bismarck unites Germany into a vast empire under Wilhelm I (1871)

Family: Look at the map "Europe 1815" in the back of *Stories of the Nations, Volume 2*, and see if the students can find Germany. Read together *Stories of the Nations, Volume 2*, chapter 2, "How Bismarck Made an Empire." Ask for an oral narration. Refer to the map "Europe before World War I, 1914" to see the large empires of Germany and Austria.

Grades 4–9: Read with your older children or assign as independent reading *Louis Pasteur*, chapter 2, "On the Verge of Mysteries." Ask for an oral or written narration.

Tip: Make sure older children are up to date with their Book of Centuries entries.

Reminder: Get the book George Mueller *for Family for lesson 15.*

Lesson 6: The Sad Story of Slavery

Materials Needed
- *Stories of America, Vol. 2*
- *Abraham Lincoln* (grades 1–3)
- *Abe Lincoln: Log Cabin to White House* (grades 4–6)
- *Lincoln: A Photobiography* (grades 7–12)
- *American Voices* (grades 10–12)

Family: Ask students what they recall about the California Gold Rush. Explain that while that was happening on the West Coast, trouble was almost ready to boil over in the rest of the country. But that trouble had a long story, and to understand it, we must go back many years to the very first colonists who came to America. Read together *Stories of America, Volume 2*, chapter 3, "The Sad Story of Slavery," and ask for an oral narration.

Grades 1–3: Ask students what they recall about Abraham's years growing up and his time on the Ohio and Mississippi Rivers. Continue reading with your younger children *Abraham Lincoln*, from where you left off ("The further south they drifted . . .") through the pranks of Abe's sons (". . . Abe only laughed at their pranks."). Ask for an oral narration.

Grades 4–6: Read with your older children or assign as independent reading *Abe Lincoln: Log Cabin to White House,* chapter 3, "The New Mother." Ask for an oral or written narration.

Grades 7–12: Read with your older children or assign as independent reading *Lincoln: A Photobiography*, chapter 4, "Half Slave and Half Free." Ask for an oral or written narration.

Grades 10–12: Also read with your older children or assign as independent reading *American Voices*, pages 177–182, "The Meaning of July Fourth for the Negro." Ask for an oral or written narration.

Reminder: Get the books Across Five Aprils *for grades 7–9 and* The Red Badge of Courage *for grades 10–12 for lesson 16.*

 # Lesson 7: How Lincoln Became President

Materials Needed
- *Stories of America, Vol. 2*
- *Our Country's Presidents*
- *Abraham Lincoln* (grades 1–3)
- *Abe Lincoln: Log Cabin to White House* (grades 4–6)
- *Lincoln: A Photobiography* (grades 7–12)
- *American Voices* (grades 10–12)

*Book of Centuries
Timeline*

*Abraham Lincoln, president during
Civil War (1809–1865)*

Family: Ask students what they recall about the issue of slavery in America. Explain that the man they have been reading about, Abraham Lincoln, played a big part in bringing about an end to slavery here. Read together *Stories of America, Volume 2*, chapter 4, "How Lincoln Became President," and ask for an oral narration. Also read together the poem on page 31, "O Captain! My Captain!," written by Walt Whitman in honor of President Lincoln upon his assassination.

Look together at *Our Country's Presidents,* the section on Abraham Lincoln. Students have read much on this president, but the illustrations and photographs, along with their captions, can add a lot to their studies.

Tip: Our Country's Presidents *will be a valuable reference book for your study of American history. You could simply display the pictures of the presidents as you progress through the historical events connected with them, or you could display the picture and read the photograph captions, or you might assign older students to read all the biographical sketches. You decide how best to use this tool based on the ages of your students. A listing will be given in these lesson plans for each president mentioned in the* Stories of America, Volume 2, *chapters, so you can know when to incorporate this book.*

Also please keep in mind that Grades 4–6 students will be assigned a presidential project at the end of Term 3. You may want to look ahead at lesson 151 for details and take steps to make sure you are not doing their work for them as you cover the presidents during this study.

Grades 1–3: Ask students what they recall about Abe's time in New Salem. Finish reading with your younger children *Abraham Lincoln*, from where you left off ("Many months of each year . . .") through the end of the book. Ask for an oral narration.

Grades 4–6: Read with your older children or assign as independent reading *Abe Lincoln: Log Cabin to White House,* chapter 4, "A Frontier Education." Ask for an oral or written narration.

Grades 7–12: Read with your older children or assign as independent reading *Lincoln: A Photobiography*, chapter 5, "Emancipation." Ask for an oral or written narration.

Grades 10–12: Also read with your older children or assign as independent reading *American Voices*, poems on pages 183–186 and Lincoln's "House Divided Speech" on pages 193–197. Ask for an oral or written narration on Lincoln's speech.

Lesson 8: Geography Book and 1 Peter 2

Materials Needed
- *The Tree in the Trail* OR *WorldTrek*
- Outline map of North America; labeled world map

• Bible
• *GOAL Bible Study Journal*
• *Discovering Doctrine* (grades 7–12)

Family Geography Book: Ask students what they recall from last time's reading about the tree and the Indian boy. Read together *The Tree in the Trail*, chapters 4 and 5, and ask for an oral narration OR read together *WorldTrek*, pages 16–24, and trace the Fishers' route on a map or globe.

Family Map Drill: Give each student a copy of a blank outline map of North America and encourage them to label the countries on the map. Compare their labeled countries with a labeled world map and make any necessary corrections. Then have them label two or three more countries on their maps or begin learning the Canadian provinces, copying the spelling and locations from the labeled world map.

Family Bible Study: Read together 1 Peter 2, looking for any descriptions of promises, commands, sins, or principles, as explained in your *GOAL Bible Study Journal*. Record your findings in your *GOAL Bible Study Journal*.

Tip: Older students should also be listening for doctrinal truths that they can add to their ongoing Discovering Doctrine *books.*

 Lesson 9: How China Opened Its Doors

Materials Needed
• *Stories of the Nations, Vol. 2*
• *Louis Pasteur* (grades 4–9)
• *How Should We Then Live?* OR *7 Men Who Rule the World from the Grave* (grades 10–12)

Family: Ask students what they recall about the making of the German Empire. Read together *Stories of the Nations, Volume 2*, chapter 3, "How China Opened Its Doors." Ask for an oral narration. Locate China on the world map in the back of *Stories of the Nations, Volume 2*, if desired.

Grades 4–9: Read with your older children or assign as independent reading *Louis Pasteur*, chapter 3, "Winning Marie." Ask for an oral or written narration.

Grades 10–12: Read with your older children or assign as independent reading *How Should We Then Live?*, the first half of chapter 2, "The Middle Ages," approximately pages 30–43, OR *7 Men Who Rule the World from the Grave*, chapter 1, "Biology Is Destiny: Charles Darwin." Ask for an oral or written narration.

Book of Centuries
Timeline

Suez Canal is opened (1869)

Lesson 10: Sailing through the Sand

Materials Needed
- *Stories of the Nations, Vol. 2*
- *Louis Pasteur* (grades 4–9)
- *How Should We Then Live?* OR *7 Men Who Rule the World from the Grave* (grades 10–12)

Family: Ask students what they recall about how China opened its doors. Explain that today's story takes place near the Red Sea. Locate the area on a world map as it is described in the first paragraph of today's reading. Read together *Stories of the Nations, Volume 2*, chapter 4, "Sailing through the Sand." Ask for an oral narration.

Grades 4–9: Read with your older children or assign as independent reading *Louis Pasteur*, chapter 4, "The Birth of Microbiology." Ask for an oral or written narration.

Grades 10–12: Read with your older children or assign as independent reading *How Should We Then Live?*, the last half of chapter 2, "The Middle Ages," approximately pages 43–56, OR *7 Men Who Rule the World from the Grave*, chapter 2, "Thinking Further About Science." Ask for an oral or written narration.

> *Tip:* Make sure older children are up to date with their Book of Centuries entries.

Lesson 11: The Great Civil War

Materials Needed
- *Stories of America, Vol. 2*
- *Buffalo Bill* (grades 1–3)
- *Abe Lincoln: Log Cabin to White House* (grades 4–6)
- *Lincoln: A Photobiography* (grades 7–12)
- *American Voices* (grades 10–12)

Family: Ask students what they recall about the war that occurred when Lincoln was president. Read together *Stories of America, Volume 2*, chapter 5, "The Great Civil War," and ask for an oral narration. Check the map on page 237 to see the regions affected by the battles.

U. S. Civil War (1861–1865)

Grades 1–3: Look at the map on page 00 of *Stories of America, Volume 2*, again, and point out all the territory west of Missouri. Explain that even while the Civil War was happening, other events were happening farther out West. Read with your younger children *Buffalo Bill*, pages 2–11. Ask for an oral narration.

Tip: As you read your way through Buffalo Bill, *make ample use of the maps in the front of that book.*

Grades 4–6: Read with your older children or assign as independent reading *Abe Lincoln: Log Cabin to White House,* chapter 5, "Flatboating Down the Mississippi." Ask for an oral or written narration.

Grades 7–12: Read with your older children or assign as independent reading *Lincoln: A Photobiography,* chapter 6, "This Dreadful War." Ask for an oral or written narration.

Grades 10–12: Also read with your older children or assign as independent reading *American Voices,* pages 198–204, "Abraham Lincoln's First Inaugural Address" and "Constitution of the Confederate States of America." Ask for an oral or written narration.

Reminder: Get the book The Story of Thomas A. Edison *for Family for lesson 21.*

"In God We Trust" first appears on U. S. coins (1864)

 # Lesson 12: War on Sea and Land

Materials Needed
- *Stories of America, Vol. 2*
- *Buffalo Bill* (grades 1–3)
- *Abe Lincoln: Log Cabin to White House* (grades 4–6)
- *Lincoln: A Photobiography* (grades 7–12)
- *American Voices* (grades 10–12)

Family: Ask students what they recall about the Civil War and its main battles and generals. Read together *Stories of America, Volume 2,* chapter 6, "War on Sea and Land," and ask for an oral narration.

Grades 1–3: Ask students what they recall about Buffalo Bill's childhood in the Kansas Territory. Read with your younger children *Buffalo Bill,* pages 12–20. Ask for an oral narration.

Grades 4–6: Read with your older children or assign as independent reading *Abe Lincoln: Log Cabin to White House,* chapter 6, "The Illinois Frontier." Ask for an oral or written narration.

Grades 7–12: Read with your older children or assign as independent reading *Lincoln: A Photobiography,* chapter 7, "Who Is Dead in the White House?" and the Lincoln Sampler of quotes. Ask for an oral or written narration.

Grades 10–12: Also read with your older children or assign as independent reading *American Voices,* pages 212–215 and pages 232–235. Ask for an oral or written narration on any of Lincoln's speeches read.

Book of Centuries
Timeline

Lesson 13: Geography Book and 1 Peter 3

Materials Needed
- *The Tree in the Trail* OR *WorldTrek*
- Outline map of North America; labeled world map
- Bible
- *GOAL Bible Study Journal*
- *Discovering Doctrine* (grades 7–12)

Family Geography Book: Ask students what they recall from last time's reading about the buffalo hunt and the new animals on the plains. Read together *The Tree in the Trail*, chapters 6–8, and ask for an oral narration OR read together *WorldTrek*, pages 26–34, and trace the Fishers' route on a map or globe.

Tip: Chapter 7 of The Tree in the Trail *mentions some ideas that may seem strange; i.e., the tree's knowing and talking. You may want to point out to the students that such were Indian beliefs at that time.*

Family Map Drill: Give each student a copy of a blank outline map of North America and encourage them to label the countries and provinces on the map. Compare their labeled countries with a labeled world map and make any necessary corrections. Then have them label two or three more countries on their maps or work on learning the Canadian provinces, copying the spelling and locations from the labeled world map.

Family Bible Study: Read together 1 Peter 3, looking for any descriptions of promises, commands, sins, or principles, as explained in your *GOAL Bible Study Journal*. Record your findings in your *GOAL Bible Study Journal*.

Tip: Older students should also be listening for doctrinal truths that they can add to their ongoing Discovering Doctrine *books.*

Lesson 14: A Tower of Air and Iron

Materials Needed
- *Stories of the Nations, Vol. 2*
- *Louis Pasteur* (grades 4–9)

Family: Ask students what they recall about the building of the Suez Canal. Read together *Stories of the Nations, Volume 2*, chapter 5, "A Tower of Air and Iron." Ask for an oral narration.

Grades 4–9: Read with your older children or assign as independent reading *Louis Pasteur*, chapter 5, "Only from Life Arises Life." Ask for an oral or written narration.

Eiffel Tower exhibited at the World Fair (1889)

Lesson 15: George Mueller, part 1

Materials Needed
- *George Mueller*
- *Louis Pasteur* (grades 4–9)
- *How Should We Then Live?* OR *7 Men Who Rule the World from the Grave* (grades 10–12)

Family: Review what students have read so far by asking them to tell a little about each of the following: Bismarck working to build Germany, China opening its doors, the Suez Canal, and the Eiffel Tower. Explain that while all those events were happening, a Christian man in England was helping thousands of children. You will read his story over the next several weeks. Read together *George Mueller*, chapter 1. Ask for an oral narration if desired.

Grades 4–9: Read with your older children or assign as independent reading *Louis Pasteur*, chapter 6, "Pasteur's Choice: To Benefit Mankind." Ask for an oral or written narration.

Grades 10–12: Read with your older children or assign as independent reading *How Should We Then Live?*, the first half of chapter 3, "The Renaissance," approximately pages 57–67, OR *7 Men Who Rule the World from the Grave*, chapter 3, "Social Darwinism." Ask for an oral or written narration.

 # Lesson 16: After the Civil War

Materials Needed
- *Stories of America, Vol. 2*
- *Buffalo Bill* (grades 1–3)
- *Abe Lincoln: Log Cabin to White House* (grades 4–6)
- *Across Five Aprils* (grades 7–9)
- *The Red Badge of Courage* (grades 10–12)
- *American Voices* (grades 10–12)

Family: Ask students what they recall about the Civil War. Explain that today they will find out a little of what happened in America after that dreadful war. Read together *Stories of America, Volume 2*, chapter 7, "After the Civil War," and ask for an oral narration.

Grades 1–3: Ask students what they recall about Buffalo Bill and the plainsmen. Read with your younger children *Buffalo Bill*, pages 21–30. Ask for an oral narration.

Grades 4–6: Read with your older children or assign as independent reading *Abe Lincoln: Log Cabin to White House*, chapter 7, "New Salem and the Black Hawk War." Ask for an oral or written narration.

Grades 7–9: Read with your older children or assign as independent

---

Book of Centuries Timeline

George Mueller provides faith-based orphanages in England (1835–1898)

U. S. purchases Alaska from Russia (1867)

reading *Across Five Aprils,* chapter 1. Ask for an oral or written narration.

Grades 10–12: Read with your older children or assign as independent reading *The Red Badge of Courage,* chapters 1 and 2. Ask for an oral or written narration.

Also read with your older children or assign as independent reading *American Voices,* pages 236–238, hymns of the era.

Custer battles Sitting Bull (1876)

Lesson 17: Custer Battles Sitting Bull

Materials Needed
- *Stories of America, Vol. 2*
- *Buffalo Bill* (grades 1–3)
- *Abe Lincoln: Log Cabin to White House* (grades 4–6)
- *Across Five Aprils* (grades 7–9)
- *The Red Badge of Courage* (grades 10–12)
- *American Voices* (grades 10–12)

Family: Ask students what they recall about the years after the Civil War. Read together *Stories of America, Volume 2,* chapter 8, "Custer Battles Sitting Bull," and ask for an oral narration.

Grades 1–3: Ask students what they recall about Buffalo Bill with the Pony Express and his experiences with trains. Read with your younger children *Buffalo Bill,* pages 31–40. Ask for an oral narration.

Grades 4–6: Read with your older children or assign as independent reading *Abe Lincoln: Log Cabin to White House,* chapter 8, "Jack of All Trades." Ask for an oral or written narration.

Grades 7–9: Read with your older children or assign as independent reading *Across Five Aprils,* chapter 2. Ask for an oral or written narration.

Grades 10–12: Read with your older children or assign as independent reading *The Red Badge of Courage,* chapters 3 and 4. Ask for an oral or written narration.

Also read with your older children or assign as independent reading *American Voices,* pages 239 and 240, more poetry of the era.

Tip: Make sure older children are up to date with their Book of Centuries entries.

Lesson 18: Geography Book and 1 Peter 4

Materials Needed
- *The Tree in the Trail* OR *WorldTrek*

- Outline map of North America; labeled world map
- Bible
- *GOAL Bible Study Journal*
- *Discovering Doctrine* (grades 7–12)

Family Geography Book: Ask students what they recall from last time's reading about the Spaniards, Comanches, and Pawnees who visited the tree. Read together *The Tree in the Trail*, chapters 9 and 10, and ask for an oral narration OR read together *WorldTrek*, pages 34–44, and trace the Fishers' route on a map or globe.

Family Map Drill: Give each student a copy of a blank outline map of North America and encourage them to label the countries and provinces on the map. Compare their labeled countries with a labeled world map and make any necessary corrections. Then have them label two or three more countries on their maps or work on learning the Canadian provinces, copying the spelling and locations from the labeled world map.

Family Bible Study: Read together 1 Peter 4, looking for any descriptions of promises, commands, sins, or principles, as explained in your *GOAL Bible Study Journal*. Record your findings in your *GOAL Bible Study Journal*.

Tip: Older students should also be listening for doctrinal truths that they can add to their ongoing Discovering Doctrine *books.*

 # Lesson 19: George Mueller, part 2

Materials Needed
- *George Mueller*
- *Louis Pasteur* (grades 4–9)
- *How Should We Then Live?* OR *7 Men Who Rule the World from the Grave* (grades 10–12)

Family: Ask what students recall from last time's reading about George Mueller and his less than stellar past. Read together *George Mueller*, chapter 2. Ask for an oral narration if desired.

Grades 4–9: Read with your older children or assign as independent reading *Louis Pasteur*, chapter 7, "Disease in the Golden Trees." Ask for an oral or written narration.

Grades 10–12: Read with your older children or assign as independent reading *How Should We Then Live?*, the last half of chapter 3, "The Renaissance," approximately pages 67–78, OR *7 Men Who Rule the World from the Grave*, the first half of chapter 4, "The Ruling Principle for All Humanity: Karl Marx," approximately pages 55–67. Ask for an oral or written narration.

Book of Centuries Timeline

Lesson 20: George Mueller, part 3

Materials Needed
- *George Mueller*
- *Louis Pasteur* (grades 4–9)

Family: Ask what students recall from last time's reading about George Mueller attending the prayer meetings. Read together *George Mueller*, chapter 3. Ask for an oral narration if desired.

Grades 4–9: Read with your older children or assign as independent reading *Louis Pasteur*, chapter 8, "So Much Still to Do." Ask for an oral or written narration.

Lesson 21: Edison: Early Years

Materials Needed
- *The Story of Thomas A. Edison*
- *Abe Lincoln: Log Cabin to White House* (grades 4–6)
- *Across Five Aprils* (grades 7–9)
- *The Red Badge of Courage* (grades 10–12)
- *American Voices* (grades 10–12)

Thomas Edison, inventor of the phonograph, light bulb, etc. (1847–1931)

Family: Ask students what they recall about Custer and his battle against Sitting Bull. Discuss how life out West was vastly different from life in the East. Help students understand how the longer people lived in an area, the more they settled in and soon had time to spend on other things, not just survival. Explain how many of the inventions of that time were thought of and designed in the East where towns and cities were already established and thriving. Read together *The Story of Thomas A. Edison*, chapters 1 and 2, "Early Years" and "Youthful Business Ventures," and ask for an oral narration.

Grades 4–6: Read with your older children or assign as independent reading *Abe Lincoln: Log Cabin to White House,* chapter 9, "Early Days in Springfield." Ask for an oral or written narration.

Grades 7–9: Read with your older children or assign as independent reading *Across Five Aprils,* chapter 3. Ask for an oral or written narration.

Grades 10–12: Read with your older children or assign as independent reading *The Red Badge of Courage,* chapters 5 and 6. Ask for an oral or written narration.

Also read with your older children or assign as independent reading *American Voices*, pages 241–243, selected hymns of the era.

Lesson 22: Edison: Study

Materials Needed
- *The Story of Thomas A. Edison*

- *Abe Lincoln: Log Cabin to White House* (grades 4–6)
- *Across Five Aprils* (grades 7–9)
- *The Red Badge of Courage* (grades 10–12)
- *American Voices* (grades 10–12)

Family: Ask students what they recall about Edison's younger years. Read together *The Story of Thomas A. Edison*, chapters 3 and 4, "Study" and "A Change of Business," and ask for an oral narration.

Grades 4–6: Read with your older children or assign as independent reading *Abe Lincoln: Log Cabin to White House*, the first half of chapter 10, "Congressman and Lawyer," pages 101–109. Ask for an oral or written narration.

Grades 7–9: Read with your older children or assign as independent reading *Across Five Aprils*, chapter 4. Ask for an oral or written narration.

Grades 10–12: Read with your older children or assign as independent reading *The Red Badge of Courage*, chapters 7 and 8. Ask for an oral or written narration.

Also read with your older children or assign as independent reading *American Voices*, pages 244 and 245, more hymns of the era.

Reminder: Get the book Sarah, Plain and Tall *for grades 1–3 for lesson 32.*

Lesson 23: Geography Book and 1 Peter 5

Materials Needed
- *The Tree in the Trail* OR *WorldTrek*
- Outline map of North America; labeled world map
- Bible
- *GOAL Bible Study Journal*
- *Discovering Doctrine* (grades 7–12)

Family Geography Book: Ask students what they recall from last time's reading about trappers and the Santa Fe Trail. Read together *The Tree in the Trail*, chapters 11–13, and ask for an oral narration OR read together *WorldTrek*, pages 45–55, and trace the Fishers' route on a map or globe.

Family Map Drill: Give each student a copy of a blank outline map of North America and encourage them to label the countries and provinces on the map. Compare their labeled countries with a labeled world map and make any necessary corrections. Then have them label two or three more countries on their maps or work on learning the Canadian provinces, copying the spelling and locations from the labeled world map.

Book of Centuries Timeline

Family Bible Study: Read together 1 Peter 5, looking for any descriptions of promises, commands, sins, or principles, as explained in your *GOAL Bible Study Journal*. Record your findings in your *GOAL Bible Study Journal*.

Tip: Older students should also be listening for doctrinal truths that they can add to their ongoing Discovering Doctrine *books.*

Lesson 24: George Mueller, part 4

Materials Needed
- *George Mueller*
- *Louis Pasteur* (grades 4–9)
- *How Should We Then Live?* OR *7 Men Who Rule the World from the Grave* (grades 10–12)

Family: Ask what students recall from last time's reading about George Mueller and his talks with Ermegarde and his father. Read together *George Mueller*, chapter 4. Ask for an oral narration if desired.

Grades 4–9: Read with your older children or assign as independent reading *Louis Pasteur*, chapter 9, "Warning: Germs Are Deadly." Ask for an oral or written narration.

Grades 10–12: Read with your older children or assign as independent reading *How Should We Then Live?,* the first half of chapter 4, "The Reformation," approximately pages 79–88, OR *7 Men Who Rule the World from the Grave,* the last half of chapter 4, "The Ruling Principle for All Humanity: Karl Marx," approximately pages 68–77. Ask for an oral or written narration.

Lesson 25: George Mueller, part 5

Materials Needed
- *George Mueller*
- *Louis Pasteur* (grades 4–9)
- *How Should We Then Live?* OR *7 Men Who Rule the World from the Grave* (grades 10–12)

Family: Ask what students recall from last time's reading about George Mueller and his plans to go to London. Read together *George Mueller*, chapter 5. Ask for an oral narration if desired.

Grades 4–9: Read with your older children or assign as independent reading *Louis Pasteur*, chapter 10, "What Is Killing our Sheep?" Ask for an oral or written narration.

Grades 10–12: Read with your older children or assign as independent reading *How Should We Then Live?,* the last half of chapter 4, "The Reformation," approximately pages 88–104, OR *7 Men Who Rule the World from the Grave,* chapter 5, "Thinking Further About Marxism." Ask for an oral or written narration.

 **Lesson 26: Edison: The Boy Telegraph Operator**

Materials Needed
  • *The Story of Thomas A. Edison*
  • *Abe Lincoln: Log Cabin to White House* (grades 4–6)
  • *Across Five Aprils* (grades 7–9)
  • *The Red Badge of Courage* (grades 10–12)
  • *American Voices* (grades 10–12)

Family: Ask students what they recall about Edison's beginning business ventures. If needed, discuss what a telegraph was and how it worked. Read together *The Story of Thomas A. Edison,* chapters 5 and 6, "The Boy Telegraph Operator" and "Telegrapher and Inventor," and ask for an oral narration.

Grades 4–6: Read with your older children or assign as independent reading *Abe Lincoln: Log Cabin to White House,* the last half of chapter 10, "Congressman and Lawyer," pages 110–118. Ask for an oral or written narration.

Grades 7–9: Read with your older children or assign as independent reading *Across Five Aprils,* chapter 5. Ask for an oral or written narration.

Grades 10–12: Read with your older children or assign as independent reading *The Red Badge of Courage,* chapters 9 and 10. Ask for an oral or written narration.

   Also read with your older children or assign as independent reading *American Voices,* pages 247 and 248, two more hymns from this time period.

Reminder: Get the book Always Inventing *for grades 4–6 for lesson 36.*

 Lesson 27: Edison: In Boston

Materials Needed
  • *The Story of Thomas A. Edison*
  • *Abe Lincoln: Log Cabin to White House* (grades 4–6)
  • *Across Five Aprils* (grades 7–9)
  • *The Red Badge of Courage* (grades 10–12)

Family: Ask students what they recall about Edison as a telegrapher. Read together *The Story of Thomas A. Edison*, chapters 7 and 8, "In Boston" and "Recognized as an Electrician," and ask for an oral narration.

Grades 4–6: Read with your older children or assign as independent reading *Abe Lincoln: Log Cabin to White House,* the first half of chapter 11, "A House Divided," pages 119–128. Ask for an oral or written narration.

Grades 7–9: Read with your older children or assign as independent reading *Across Five Aprils,* chapter 6. Ask for an oral or written narration.

Grades 10–12: Read with your older children or assign as independent reading *The Red Badge of Courage,* chapters 11 and 12. Ask for an oral or written narration.

Tip: Make sure older children are up to date with their Book of Centuries entries.

Lesson 28: Geography Book and 2 Peter 1

Materials Needed
- *The Tree in the Trail* OR *WorldTrek*
- Outline map of North America; labeled world map
- Bible
- *GOAL Bible Study Journal*
- *Discovering Doctrine* (grades 7–12)

Family Geography Book: Ask students what they recall from last time's reading about Jed's introduction to the tree. Read together *The Tree in the Trail*, chapters 14 and 15, and ask for an oral narration OR read together *WorldTrek*, pages 55–59, and trace the Fishers' route on a map or globe.

Family Map Drill: Give each student a copy of a blank outline map of North America and encourage them to label the countries and provinces on the map. Compare their labeled countries with a labeled world map and make any necessary corrections. Then have them label two or three more countries on their maps or work on learning the Canadian provinces, copying the spelling and locations from the labeled world map.

Family Bible Study: Read together 2 Peter 1, looking for any descriptions of promises, commands, sins, or principles, as explained in your *GOAL Bible Study Journal*. Record your findings in your *GOAL Bible Study Journal*.

Tip: Older students should also be listening for doctrinal truths that they can add to their ongoing Discovering Doctrine books.

Lesson 29: George Mueller, part 6

Materials Needed
- *George Mueller*
- *Louis Pasteur* (grades 4–9)

Family: Ask what students recall from last time's reading about George Mueller and his time with the London Society. Read together *George Mueller*, chapter 6. Ask for an oral narration if desired.

Grades 4–9: Read with your older children or assign as independent reading *Louis Pasteur*, chapter 11, "Solving the Mystery of Vaccination." Ask for an oral or written narration.

 ## Lesson 30: George Mueller, part 7

Materials Needed
- *George Mueller*
- *Louis Pasteur* (grades 4–9)
- *How Should We Then Live?* OR *7 Men Who Rule the World from the Grave* (grades 10–12)

Family: Ask what students recall from last time's reading about George Mueller and his new wife and church. Read together *George Mueller*, chapter 7. Ask for an oral narration if desired.

Grades 4–9: Read with your older children or assign as independent reading *Louis Pasteur*, chapter 12, "All France Awaits the Results." Ask for an oral or written narration.

Grades 10–12: Read with your older children or assign as independent reading *How Should We Then Live?,* chapter 5, "The Reformation—Continued," OR *7 Men Who Rule the World from the Grave,* the first half of chapter 6, "Closing the Book: Julius Wellhausen," approximately pages 89–98. Ask for an oral or written narration.

Reminder: Get the book Rescue and Redeem *for grades 7–12 for lesson 40.*

 ## Lesson 31: Edison: Inventor and Manufacturer

Materials Needed
- *The Story of Thomas A. Edison*
- *Abe Lincoln: Log Cabin to White House* (grades 4–6)

• *Across Five Aprils* (grades 7–9)
• *The Red Badge of Courage* (grades 10–12)
• *American Voices* (grades 10–12)

Family: Ask students what they recall about Edison's time in Boston, Massachusetts. Read together *The Story of Thomas A. Edison,* chapters 9 and 10, "Inventor and Manufacturer" and "The Wizard of Menlo Park," and ask for an oral narration.

Grades 4–6: Read with your older children or assign as independent reading *Abe Lincoln: Log Cabin to White House,* the last half of chapter 11, "A House Divided," pages 129–139. Ask for an oral or written narration.

Grades 7–9: Read with your older children or assign as independent reading *Across Five Aprils,* chapter 7. Ask for an oral or written narration.

Grades 10–12: Read with your older children or assign as independent reading *The Red Badge of Courage,* chapters 13 and 14. Ask for an oral or written narration.

Also read with your older children or assign as independent reading *American Voices,* hymns on pages 249 and 250.

 # Lesson 32: Edison: Inventions

Materials Needed
• *The Story of Thomas A. Edison*
• *Sarah, Plain and Tall* (grades 1–3)
• *Abe Lincoln: Log Cabin to White House* (grades 4–6)
• *Across Five Aprils* (grades 7–9)
• *The Red Badge of Courage* (grades 10–12)
• *American Voices* (grades 10–12)

Family: Ask students what they recall about Edison's time in Menlo Park. Read together *The Story of Thomas A. Edison,* chapters 11 and 12, "Inventions" and "At Orange, New Jersey," and ask for an oral narration. Also read together the Afterword and look through the Appendix as desired.

Grades 1–3: Explain that while Thomas Edison was working and inventing in the East, different stories were happening out on the plains in the West. Read with your younger children *Sarah, Plain and Tall,* chapter 1.

Grades 4–6: Read with your older children or assign as independent reading *Abe Lincoln: Log Cabin to White House,* chapter 12, "With Malice Toward None." Ask for an oral or written narration.

Grades 7–9: Read with your older children or assign as independent reading *Across Five Aprils,* chapter 8. Ask for an oral or written narration.

Grades 10–12: Read with your older children or assign as independent

reading *The Red Badge of Courage,* chapters 15 and 16. Ask for an oral or written narration.

Also read with your older children or assign as independent reading *American Voices,* pages 251 and 252, "Casey at the Bat."

Reminder: Get the book Bully for You, Teddy Roosevelt *for grades 7–12 for lesson 42.*

Lesson 33: Geography Book and 2 Peter 2

Materials Needed
- *The Tree in the Trail* OR *WorldTrek*
- Outline map of North America; labeled world map
- Bible
- *GOAL Bible Study Journal*
- *Discovering Doctrine* (grades 7–12)

Family Geography Book: Ask students what they recall from last time's reading about the tree's death. Read together *The Tree in the Trail,* chapters 16–18, and ask for an oral narration OR read together *WorldTrek,* pages 59–62, and trace the Fishers' route on a map or globe.

Family Map Drill: Give each student a copy of a blank outline map of North America and encourage them to label the countries and provinces on the map. Compare their labeled countries with a labeled world map and make any necessary corrections. Then have them label two or three more countries on their maps or work on learning the Canadian provinces, copying the spelling and locations from the labeled world map.

Family Bible Study: Read together 2 Peter 2, looking for any descriptions of promises, commands, sins, or principles, as explained in your *GOAL Bible Study Journal.* Record your findings in your *GOAL Bible Study Journal.*

Tip: Older students should also be listening for doctrinal truths that they can add to their ongoing Discovering Doctrine *books.*

 # Lesson 34: George Mueller, part 8

Materials Needed
- *George Mueller*
- *Louis Pasteur* (grades 4–9)
- *How Should We Then Live?* OR *7 Men Who Rule the World from the Grave* (grades 10–12)

*Book of Centuries
Timeline*

Family: Ask what students recall from last time's reading about George Mueller and learning to trust God for money. Read together *George Mueller*, chapter 8. Ask for an oral narration if desired.

Grades 4–9: Read with your older children or assign as independent reading *Louis Pasteur*, chapter 13, "The Conquest of Rabies." Ask for an oral or written narration.

Grades 10–12: Read with your older children or assign as independent reading *How Should We Then Live?*, chapter 6, "The Enlightenment," OR *7 Men Who Rule the World from the Grave*, the last half of chapter 6, "Closing the Book: Julius Wellhausen," approximately pages 98–104. Ask for an oral or written narration.

⊢⊣ Lesson 35: George Mueller, part 9

Materials Needed
 • *George Mueller*
 • *Louis Pasteur* (grades 4–9)

Family: Ask what students recall from last time's reading about George Mueller and his first time ministering in the slums. Read together *George Mueller*, chapter 9. Ask for an oral narration if desired.

Grades 4–9: Read with your older children or assign as independent reading *Louis Pasteur*, chapter 14, "I Have Done What I Could." Ask for an oral or written narration.

Reminder: Get the book The Singing Tree *for grades 4–6 for lesson 45.*

Lesson 36: Mr. Bell Invents the Telephone

Materials Needed
 • *Stories of America, Vol. 2*
 • *Sarah, Plain and Tall* (grades 1–3)
 • *Always Inventing* (grades 4–6)
 • *Across Five Aprils* (grades 7–9)
 • *The Red Badge of Courage* (grades 10–12)
 • *American Voices* (grades 10–12)

Alexander Graham Bell invents the telephone (1876)

Family: Ask students what they recall about Edison's inventions. Explain that Thomas Edison was not the only person inventing and improving things. Read together *Stories of America, Volume 2*, chapter 9, "Mr. Bell Invents the Telephone," and ask for an oral narration.

Grades 1–3: Read with your younger children *Sarah, Plain and Tall,* chapter 2.

Grades 4–6: Read with your older children or assign as independent reading *Always Inventing,* pages 8–13. Ask for an oral or written narration.

Grades 7–9: Read with your older children or assign as independent reading *Across Five Aprils,* chapter 9. Ask for an oral or written narration.

Grades 10–12: Read with your older children or assign as independent reading *The Red Badge of Courage,* chapters 17 and 18. Ask for an oral or written narration.

Also read with your older children or assign as independent reading *American Voices,* page 253, "Faith Is the Victory."

Lesson 37: The Right to Vote

Materials Needed
- *Stories of America, Vol. 2*
- *Sarah, Plain and Tall* (grades 1–3)
- *Always Inventing* (grades 4–6)
- *Across Five Aprils* (grades 7–9)
- *The Red Badge of Courage* (grades 10–12)
- *American Voices* (grades 10–12)

Family: Ask students what they recall about Alexander Graham Bell. Explain that while some people worked to change items used in everyday life, others were working to change our country's laws. Read together *Stories of America, Volume 2,* chapter 10, "The Right to Vote," and ask for an oral narration.

Grades 1–3: Read with your younger children *Sarah, Plain and Tall,* chapter 3.

Grades 4–6: Read with your older children or assign as independent reading *Always Inventing,* pages 14–23. Ask for an oral or written narration.

Grades 7–9: Read with your older children or assign as independent reading *Across Five Aprils,* chapter 10. Ask for an oral or written narration.

Grades 10–12: Read with your older children or assign as independent reading *The Red Badge of Courage,* chapters 19–21. Ask for an oral or written narration.

Also read with your older children or assign as independent reading *American Voices,* pages 143–145, "Seneca Falls Declaration." Ask for an oral or written narration.

Seneca Falls Convention for women's suffrage (1848)

Nineteenth amendment grants women the right to vote (1920)

Tip: Make sure older children are up to date with their Book of Centuries entries.

Lesson 38: Geography Book and 2 Peter 3

Materials Needed
- *The Tree in the Trail* OR *WorldTrek*
- Outline map of North America; labeled world map
- Bible
- *GOAL Bible Study Journal*
- *Discovering Doctrine* (grades 7–12)

Family Geography Book: Ask students what they recall from last time's reading about what Jed made from the tree. Read together *The Tree in the Trail*, chapters 19 and 20, and ask for an oral narration OR read together *WorldTrek*, pages 63–70, and trace the Fishers' route on a map or globe.

Family Map Drill: Give each student a copy of a blank outline map of North America and encourage them to label the countries and provinces on the map. Compare their labeled countries with a labeled world map and make any necessary corrections. Then have them label two or three more countries on their maps or work on learning the Canadian provinces, copying the spelling and locations from the labeled world map.

Family Bible Study: Read together 2 Peter 3, looking for any descriptions of promises, commands, sins, or principles, as explained in your *GOAL Bible Study Journal*. Record your findings in your *GOAL Bible Study Journal*.

Tip: Older students should also be listening for doctrinal truths that they can add to their ongoing Discovering Doctrine *books.*

Lesson 39: George Mueller, part 10

Materials Needed
- *George Mueller*
- *Louis Pasteur* (grades 4–9)
- *How Should We Then Live?* (grades 10–12)

Family: Ask what students recall from last time's reading about George Mueller's idea for an orphanage. Read together *George Mueller*, chapter 10. Ask for an oral narration if desired.

Grades 4–9: Read with your older children or assign as independent reading *Louis Pasteur*, chapter 15, "Louis Pasteur in Today's World." Ask for an oral or written narration.

Grades 10–12: Read with your older children or assign as independent reading *How Should We Then Live?,* chapter 7, "The Rise of Modern Science." Ask for an oral or written narration. Students who are reading *7 Men Who*

Rule the World from the Grave have no assignment today.

Tip: Older students will take a break from How Should We Then Live? *and* 7 Men Who Rule the World from the Grave *here. The readings have brought them up to the current time period being studied. Both books will be finished later in the year after modern history has been read.*

Lesson 40: George Mueller, part 11

Materials Needed
- *George Mueller*
- *Rescue and Redeem* (grades 7–12)

Family: Ask what students recall from last time's reading about George Mueller and the start of his orphanage. Read together *George Mueller*, chapter 11. Ask for an oral narration if desired.

Grades 7–12: Read with your older children or assign as independent reading *Rescue and Redeem*, pages 11–16, "What is the Modern Church?" Ask for an oral or written narration.

Lesson 41: Booker T. Washington

Materials Needed
- *Stories of America, Vol. 2*
- *Sarah, Plain and Tall* (grades 1–3)
- *Always Inventing* (grades 4–6)
- *Across Five Aprils* (grades 7–9)
- *The Red Badge of Courage* (grades 10–12)
- *American Voices* (grades 10–12)

Booker T. Washington rises from slavery to leader of Tuskegee Institute (1856–1915)

Family: Ask students what they recall about suffrage and the laws Elizabeth Stanton and Susan B. Anthony were trying to change. Explain that another group of people were also struggling: those who had been slaves before Abraham Lincoln set them free. In those days they were called "colored" people, and rarely did they have opportunity for an education. Read together *Stories of America, Volume 2*, chapter 11, "Booker T. Washington," and ask for an oral narration.

Grades 1–3: Read with your younger children *Sarah, Plain and Tall*, chapter 4.

Grades 4–6: Read with your older children or assign as independent reading *Always Inventing*, pages 24–27. Ask for an oral or written narration.

*Book of Centuries
Timeline*

Grades 7–9: Read with your older children or assign as independent reading *Across Five Aprils,* chapters 11 and 12. Ask for an oral or written narration.

Grades 10–12: Read with your older children or assign as independent reading *The Red Badge of Courage,* chapters 22–24. Ask for an oral or written narration.

Also read with your older children or assign as independent reading *American Voices,* pages 275–277, "Speech Before the Atlanta Cotton States and International Exposition." Ask for an oral or written narration.

Tip: If your grades 7–12 students would like to read more about Booker T. Washington, give them Up From Slavery, *his autobiography.*

 # Lesson 42: Lady Liberty

Materials Needed
- *Stories of America, Vol. 2*
- *Our Country's Presidents*
- *Sarah, Plain and Tall* (grades 1–3)
- *Always Inventing* (grades 4–6)
- *Bully for You, Teddy Roosevelt* (grades 7–12)
- *American Voices* (grades 10–12)

Family: For a quick review, mention each of the following names or events, one at a time, and ask students what they remember about them: Oregon Trail, California Gold Rush, Abraham Lincoln, Civil War, General Custer, Thomas Edison, Alexander Graham Bell, Booker T. Washington. Read together *Stories of America, Volume 2,* chapter 12, "Lady Liberty," and ask for an oral narration. Also read together the poem that is displayed with the Statue of Liberty, "The New Colossus," on page 79.

Look together at *Our Country's Presidents,* the section on Grover Cleveland, who was president when the Statue of Liberty was installed.

Statue of Liberty erected in New York Harbor (1886)

Grades 1–3: Read with your younger children *Sarah, Plain and Tall,* chapter 5.

Grades 4–6: Read with your older children or assign as independent reading *Always Inventing,* pages 28–37. Ask for an oral or written narration.

Grades 7–12: Read with your older children or assign as independent reading *Bully for You, Teddy Roosevelt,* chapter 1. Ask for an oral or written narration.

Grades 10–12: Also read with your older children or assign as independent reading *American Voices,* pages 285–292, "Of Booker T. Washington and Others." Ask for an oral or written narration.

Reminder: Get the book The Brooklyn Bridge *for Family for lesson 52.*

Lesson 43: Geography Book and Jude

Materials Needed
- *The Tree in the Trail* OR *WorldTrek*
- Outline map of North America; labeled world map
- Bible
- *GOAL Bible Study Journal*
- *Discovering Doctrine* (grades 7–12)

Family Geography Book: Ask students what they recall from last time's reading about the yoke's travels. Read together *The Tree in the Trail*, chapters 21–23, and ask for an oral narration OR read together *WorldTrek*, pages 70–79, and trace the Fishers' route on a map or globe.

Family Map Drill: Give each student a copy of a blank outline map of North America and encourage them to label the countries and provinces on the map. Compare their labeled countries with a labeled world map and make any necessary corrections. Then have them label two or three more countries on their maps or work on learning the Canadian provinces, copying the spelling and locations from the labeled world map.

Family Bible Study: Read together Jude, looking for any descriptions of promises, commands, sins, or principles, as explained in your *GOAL Bible Study Journal*. Record your findings in your *GOAL Bible Study Journal*.

Tip: Older students should also be listening for doctrinal truths that they can add to their ongoing Discovering Doctrine *books.*

Lesson 44: George Mueller, part 12

Materials Needed
- *George Mueller*
- *Rescue and Redeem* (grades 7–12)

Family: Ask what students recall from last time's reading about George Mueller and God's faithfulness to him. Read together *George Mueller*, chapter 12. Ask for an oral narration if desired.

Grades 7–12: Read with your older children or assign as independent reading *Rescue and Redeem,* pages 17–37, "Niijima Jo." Ask for an oral or written narration.

Lesson 45: George Mueller, part 13

Materials Needed
- *George Mueller*
- *The Singing Tree* (grades 4–6)
- *Rescue and Redeem* (grades 7–12)

Family: Ask what students recall from last time's reading about George Mueller and how the orphanage grew. Read together *George Mueller*, chapter 13. Ask for an oral narration if desired.

Grades 4–6: Read with your older children or assign as independent reading *The Singing Tree*, chapter 1, "Uncle Moses."

Grades 7–12: Read with your older children or assign as independent reading *Rescue and Redeem*, pages 39–62, "Missions in a Modern World" and "Hudson and Maria Taylor." Ask for an oral or written narration.

 Lesson 46: Helen Keller

Materials Needed
- *Stories of America, Vol. 2*
- *Sarah, Plain and Tall* (grades 1–3)
- *Always Inventing* (grades 4–6)
- *Bully for You, Teddy Roosevelt* (grades 7–12)

Family: Ask students what they recall about the Statue of Liberty. Explain that today's story is about a little girl and her very patient teacher. Read together *Stories of America, Volume 2*, chapter 13, "Helen Keller," and ask for an oral narration.

Grades 1–3: Read with your younger children *Sarah, Plain and Tall*, chapter 6.

Grades 4–6: Read with your older children or assign as independent reading *Always Inventing*, pages 38–43. Ask for an oral or written narration.

Grades 7–12: Read with your older children or assign as independent reading *Bully for You, Teddy Roosevelt*, chapter 2. Ask for an oral or written narration.

Tip: If your grades 7–12 students would like to read more about Helen Keller, give them The Story of My Life*, her autobiography.*

Helen Keller, deaf and blind, communicates with the world through Anne Sullivan (1880–1968)

 Lesson 47: The Spanish-American War

Materials Needed
- *Stories of America, Vol. 2*

• *Sarah, Plain and Tall* (grades 1–3)
• *Always Inventing* (grades 4–6)
• *Bully for You, Teddy Roosevelt* (grades 7–12)

Family: Ask students what they recall about Helen Keller. Explain that America went to war again during Helen Keller's lifetime. Read together *Stories of America, Volume 2*, chapter 14, "The Spanish-American War," and ask for an oral narration.

Grades 1–3: Read with your younger children *Sarah, Plain and Tall*, chapter 7.

Grades 4–6: Read with your older children or assign as independent reading *Always Inventing*, pages 44–57. Ask for an oral or written narration.

Grades 7–12: Read with your older children or assign as independent reading *Bully for You, Teddy Roosevelt*, chapter 3. Ask for an oral or written narration.

Tip: Make sure older children are up to date with their Book of Centuries entries.

Reminder: Start gathering the resources you will need for Term 2. See pages 61 and 62.

Reminder: If you want to do the optional hands-on project for lesson 56, start collecting the materials you will need.

Lesson 48: Geography Book and 1 John 1

Materials Needed
• *The Tree in the Trail* OR *WorldTrek*
• Outline map of North America; labeled world map
• Bible
• *GOAL Bible Study Journal*
• *Discovering Doctrine* (grades 7–12)

Family Geography Book: Ask students what they recall from last time's reading about the trip on the Santa Fe trail. Read together *The Tree in the Trail*, chapters 24 and 25, and ask for an oral narration OR read together *WorldTrek*, pages 79–85, and trace the Fishers' route on a map or globe.

Family Map Drill: Give each student a copy of a blank outline map of North America and encourage them to label the countries and provinces on the map. Compare their labeled countries with a labeled world map and make any necessary corrections. Then have them label two or three more countries on their maps or work on learning the Canadian provinces, copying the spelling and locations from the labeled world map.

Family Bible Study: Read together 1 John 1, looking for any descriptions of promises, commands, sins, or principles, as explained in your *GOAL Bible Study Journal.* Record your findings in your *GOAL Bible Study Journal.*

Tip: Older students should also be listening for doctrinal truths that they can add to their ongoing Discovering Doctrine *books.*

 # Lesson 49: George Mueller, part 14

Materials Needed
- *George Mueller*
- *The Singing Tree* (grades 4–6)
- *Rescue and Redeem* (grades 7–12)

Family: Ask what students recall from last time's reading about George Mueller and problems with the neighbors. Read together *George Mueller,* chapter 14. Ask for an oral narration if desired.

Grades 4–6: Read with your older children or assign as independent reading *The Singing Tree,* chapter 2, "The Poplar Lane."

Grades 7–12: Read with your older children or assign as independent reading *Rescue and Redeem,* pages 63–78, "Dwight Moody and Ira Sankey." Ask for an oral or written narration.

 # Lesson 50: George Mueller, part 15

Materials Needed
- *George Mueller*
- *The Singing Tree* (grades 4–6)
- *Rescue and Redeem* (grades 7–12)

Family: Ask what students recall from last time's reading about George Mueller and the new orphanage. Read together *George Mueller,* chapter 15. Ask for an oral narration if desired.

Grades 4–6: Read with your older children or assign as independent reading *The Singing Tree,* chapter 3, "The Young Master."

Grades 7–12: Read with your older children or assign as independent reading *Rescue and Redeem,* pages 79–99, "Robert Thomas, John Ross and Samuel Moffett." Ask for an oral or written narration.

Lesson 51: Theodore Roosevelt

Materials Needed
- *Stories of America, Vol. 2*
- *Our Country's Presidents*
- *Sarah, Plain and Tall* (grades 1–3)
- *Always Inventing* (grades 4–6)
- *Bully for You, Teddy Roosevelt* (grades 7–12)
- *American Voices* (grades 10–12)

Book of Centuries Timeline

Family: Ask students what they recall about the Spanish-American War. Explain that today's story is about a man who rode with the Rough Riders in that war and later became president. Read together *Stories of America, Volume 2*, chapter 15, "Theodore Roosevelt: Rough Rider and President," and ask for an oral narration.

Look together at *Our Country's Presidents,* the section on Theodore Roosevelt. Older students are reading much on this president, but the illustrations and photographs, along with their captions, can add to their studies.

Theodore Roosevelt (1858–1919)

Grades 1–3: Read with your younger children *Sarah, Plain and Tall*, chapter 8.

Grades 4–6: Read with your older children or assign as independent reading *Always Inventing,* pages 58–60. Ask for an oral or written narration.

Grades 7–12: Read with your older children or assign as independent reading *Bully for You, Teddy Roosevelt,* chapter 4. Ask for an oral or written narration.

Grades 10–12: Also read with your older children or assign as independent reading *American Voices*, page 293, "Roosevelt Corollary to the Monroe Doctrine." Ask for an oral or written narration.

Lesson 52: The Brooklyn Bridge

Materials Needed
- *The Brooklyn Bridge*
- *Sarah, Plain and Tall* (grades 1–3)
- *Bully for You, Teddy Roosevelt* (grades 7–12)

Family: Ask students what they recall about Theodore Roosevelt. Explain that today you will read about a famous bridge that "grew up" even while Teddy Roosevelt did. Read together *The Brooklyn Bridge* and ask for an oral narration.

Brooklyn Bridge completed (1883)

Grades 1–3: Read with your younger children *Sarah, Plain and Tall*, chapter 9.

Grades 7–12: Read with your older children or assign as independent reading *Bully for You, Teddy Roosevelt,* chapter 5. Ask for an oral or written narration.

 Lesson 53: Geography Book and 1 John 2

Materials Needed
- *The Tree in the Trail* OR *WorldTrek*
- Outline map of North America; labeled world map
- Bible
- *GOAL Bible Study Journal*
- *Discovering Doctrine* (grades 7–12)

Family Geography Book: Ask students what they recall from last time's reading about the yoke's journey. Read together *The Tree in the Trail,* chapters 26 and 27, and ask for an oral narration OR read together *WorldTrek,* pages 86–92, and trace the Fishers' route on a map or globe.

Family Map Drill: Give each student a copy of a blank outline map of North America and encourage them to label the countries and provinces on the map. Compare their labeled countries with a labeled world map and make any necessary corrections.

Family Bible Study: Read together 1 John 2, looking for any descriptions of promises, commands, sins, or principles, as explained in your *GOAL Bible Study Journal.* Record your findings in your *GOAL Bible Study Journal.*

Tip: Older students should also be listening for doctrinal truths that they can add to their ongoing Discovering Doctrine *books.*

 Lesson 54: George Mueller, part 16

Materials Needed
- *George Mueller*
- *The Singing Tree* (grades 4–6)
- *Rescue and Redeem* (grades 7–12)

Family: Ask what students recall from last time's reading about George Mueller and his plans to expand. Read together *George Mueller,* chapter 16. Ask for an oral narration if desired.

Grades 4–6: Read with your older children or assign as independent reading *The Singing Tree,* chapter 4, "The Wedding."

Grades 7–12: Read with your older children or assign as independent reading *Rescue and Redeem*, pages 101–126, "Living the Golden Rule" and "Pandita Ramabai." Ask for an oral or written narration.

 # Lesson 55: George Mueller, part 17

Materials Needed
- *George Mueller*
- *The Singing Tree* (grades 4–6)
- *Rescue and Redeem* (grades 7–12)

Family: Ask what students recall from last time's reading about George Mueller and the obstacles he faced for expanding the orphanage. Read together *George Mueller*, chapter 17 and Later. Ask for an oral narration if desired.

Grades 4–6: Read with your older children or assign as independent reading *The Singing Tree,* chapter 5, "For Conspicuous Bravery."

Tip: Grades 4–6 students will finish The Singing Tree *next term.*

Grades 7–12: Read with your older children or assign as independent reading *Rescue and Redeem*, pages 127–147, "Princess Ka'iulani." Ask for an oral or written narration.

 # Lesson 56: American History Project or Exam

Materials Needed
- (optional) Materials for hands-on project
- *Bully for You, Teddy Roosevelt* (grades 7–12)

Family: Do a hands-on project (see below), or use the questions below to begin the students' exam on American history.

Tip: Exams in a Charlotte Mason school require no "cramming" or preparation. You may be pleasantly surprised

Grades 1–3: Tell the story of Abraham Lincoln.
Grades 4–6: Tell all that you remember about Abraham Lincoln and the Civil War.
Grades 7–9: In *Across Five Aprils* the editor warned Jethro, "Don't expect peace to be a perfect pearl." What did he mean, and how was that warning a fitting description of the effects of the Civil War?

Grades 10–12: Describe fully the causes of the Civil War, the events of the Civil War, and the effects of the war on America's people.

Tip: You may want to assign the older students to write their exam answers. Younger students may do oral exams; you might want to write or type their answers as they tell what they know. Or, if you have students in more than one grade level, you might allow them to do their exams orally in a group. That way the older can hear the younger, and the younger can hear the older.

Optional Hands-On Project: Select a hands-on project from the Links and Tips page: http://SimplyCharlotteMason.com/books/modern/links-tips

Grades 7–12: Read with your older children or assign as independent reading *Bully for You, Teddy Roosevelt,* chapter 6. Ask for an oral or written narration.

Lesson 57: American History Project or Exam

Materials Needed
• *Bully for You, Teddy Roosevelt* (grades 7–12)

Family: Finish your selected hands-on project, or use the questions below to continue the students' exam on American history.

Grades 1–3: Tell about a person of whom you read who invented something or made something of importance to the American people.
Grades 4–6: Select three of the following famous people and tell all you remember about them: Thomas Edison, Alexander Graham Bell, Booker T. Washington, Frederic Bartholdi, Helen Keller, Theodore Roosevelt.
Grades 7–9: Describe two challenges that faced America during the last half of the nineteenth century, besides the Civil War, and how those challenges were met.
Grades 10–12: Discuss the similarities and differences between Abraham Lincoln and Theodore Roosevelt: their childhoods, experiences before becoming president, presidential administrations, and characters.

Tip: Students in grades 10–12 should complete their reading of Bully for You, Teddy Roosevelt *before answering this exam question.*

Grades 7–12: Read with your older children or assign as independent reading *Bully for You, Teddy Roosevelt,* chapter 7. Ask for an oral or written narration.

Lesson 58: Geography and Bible Exams

Family Geography Exam: Use the questions below according to the book you have been reading.

The Tree in the Trail: Show on a map where the tree was located in America and tell about the changes that came to the country around it.

WorldTrek: Select two of the countries the Fishers have visited in the book and tell all you remember about each: Great Britain, Ireland, Norway, Sweden, Estonia, Russia, Czech Republic.

Map Drill: Give each student a copy of a blank outline map of North America and ask them to label the countries and Canadian provinces on the map.

Bible Exam: Use the questions below for the students' exam on 1 Peter, 2 Peter, and Jude.

Grades 1–3: Name two GOAL items you have found in 1 Peter, 2 Peter, or Jude and been able to do, not just hear.

Grades 4–12: Name the four things you are looking for in the Bible passages you have been reading (GOAL) and give at least one example of each from 1 Peter, 2 Peter, or Jude.

Tip: If you assigned Scripture memory from 1 Peter, 2 Peter, and Jude, you might also ask for a recitation of the passage(s). Be sure to encourage the children to say beautiful words in a beautiful way as they recite.

Lesson 59: World History Exam

Family: Use the questions below to begin the students' exam on Modern world history.

Grades 1–3: Tell the story of the Suez Canal or the Eiffel Tower.
Grades 4–6: Tell all you know about Louis Pasteur.
Grades 7–9: Describe why Louis Pasteur may be considered a founder of modern medicine. Cite examples from your reading about medical views before and after his work.
Grades 10–12: Discuss the prominent philosophies of which you read and how they contributed to a changing worldview over the years.

Lesson 60: World History Exam

Family: Use the questions below to continue the students' exam on Modern world history.

Book of Centuries Timeline

Grades 1–6: Tell the story of George Mueller.

Grades 7–9: Tell the stories of two modern missionaries of whom you read: Niijima Jo, Hudson Taylor, Dwight Moody, Robert Thomas, Pandita Ramabai, Princess Ka'iulani.

Grades 10–12: Describe missions in a modern world. How has it changed from earlier eras. Cite examples from your reading.

Term 2
(12 weeks; 5 lessons/week)

American History Resources

✓ *Stories of America, Volume 2*, by Charles Morris, et al.
- *Our Country's Presidents* by Ann Bausum (reference book)
✓ *Empire State Building* by Elizabeth Mann
✓ *Hoover Dam* by Elizabeth Mann

Grades 1–3
- *A Boy Named FDR* by Kathleen Krull
✓ *Franklin and Winston: A Christmas That Changed the World* by Douglas Wood
✓ *Rebekkah's Journey* by Ann E. Burg
- *Lily's Victory Garden* by Helen L. Wilbur
✓ *The Unbreakable Code* by Sara Hoagland Hunter

Grades 4–6
✓ *The Wright Brothers: Pioneers of American Aviation* by Quentin Reynolds

Grades 7–9
- *The Wright Brothers: How They Invented the Airplane* by Russell Freedman
- *The Yanks Are Coming* by Albert Marrin
- *Victory in the Pacific* by Albert Marrin
- Book of Centuries (one for each student)

Grades 10–12
- *The Wright Brothers: How They Invented the Airplane* by Russell Freedman
- *America: The Last Best Hope, Volume 2: From a World at War to the Triumph of Freedom* by William Bennett
- *The Yanks Are Coming* by Albert Marrin
- *Victory in the Pacific* by Albert Marrin
- *American Voices* edited by Ray Notgrass
- Book of Centuries (one for each student)

Optional Resources
- *George Washington Carver* by David Collins (grades 1–3)
- Dover coloring books
- Various resources for optional hands-on projects

World History, Bible, Geography Resources

✓ *Stories of the Nations, Volume 2*, by Lorene Lambert
- *GOAL Bible Study Journal* by Sonya Shafer
- *Come, Lord Jesus: A Revelation Bible Study* by Sonya Shafer
- Bible
✓ *Minn of the Mississippi* by Holling C. Holling
  OR *WorldTrek* by Russell and Carla Fisher
- *Uncle Josh's Outline Map book or CD* by George and Hannah Wiggers (United States)
- Labeled United States map

Grades 1–3
  ✓• *Only a Dog* by Bertha Whitridge Smith
  ✓• *The Little Ships* by Louise Borden
  • *Always Remember Me* by Marisabina Russo
  ✓• *The Journey that Saved Curious George* by Louise Borden

Grades 4–6
  ✓• *The Singing Tree* by Kate Seredy
  ✓• *Where Poppies Grow* by Linda Granfield
  ✓• *Snow Treasure* by Marie McSwigan

Grades 7–9
  • *Across America on an Emigrant Train* by Jim Murphy
  • *World War I: From the Lusitania to Versailles* by Zachary Kent
  • *The Endless Steppe* by Esther Hautzig
  • *Discovering Doctrine* by Sonya Shafer (one for each student)
  • Book of Centuries (one for each student)

Grades 10–12
  • *The War to End All Wars* by Russell Freedman
  • *Hitler* by Albert Marrin
  • *Discovering Doctrine* by Sonya Shafer (one for each student)
  • Book of Centuries (one for each student)

Optional Resources
  • *The Hiding Place* by Corrie Ten Boom (grades 10–12)
  • Dover coloring books

	Family	Grades 1–3	4–6	7–9	10–12
Week 1, Lessons 61–65					
American History	Stories of America, Vol. 2, ch. 16, 17	(opt.) George Washington Carver, ch. 1, 2	The Wright Brothers, ch. 1, 2	The Wright Brothers: How They Invented the Airplane, ch. 1–3	The Wright Brothers: How They Invented the Airplane, ch. 1–3; American Voices, p. 284
Geography	Minn of the Mississippi, ch. 1, OR WorldTrek, pp. 92–100; Map Drill: United States				
Bible	1 John 3				
World History	Stories of the Nations, ch. 6, 7		The Singing Tree, ch. 6, 7	Across America on an Emigrant Train, Intro–ch. 2	The War to End All Wars, ch. 1, 2
Week 2, Lessons 66–70					
American History	Stories of America, Vol. 2, ch. 18, 19	(opt.) George Washington Carver, ch. 3, 4	The Wright Brothers, ch. 3, 4	The Wright Brothers: How They Invented the Airplane, ch. 4, 5	The Wright Brothers: How They Invented the Airplane, ch. 4, 5
Geography	Minn of the Mississippi, ch. 2, 3, OR WorldTrek, pp. 100–104; Map Drill: United States				
Bible	1 John 4				
World History	Stories of the Nations, ch. 8, 9		The Singing Tree, ch. 8, 9	Across America on an Emigrant Train, ch. 3, 4	The War to End All Wars, ch. 3, 4
Week 3, Lessons 71–75					
American History	Stories of America, Vol. 2, ch. 20 and poem	(opt.) George Washington Carver, ch. 5, 6	The Wright Brothers, ch. 5, 6	The Wright Brothers: How They Invented the Airplane, ch. 6–8	The Wright Brothers: How They Invented the Airplane, ch. 6–8; Amer. Voices, pp. 294–296
Geography	Minn of the Mississippi, ch. 4, 5, OR WorldTrek, pp. 104–111; Map Drill: United States				
Bible	1 John 5				
World History	Stories of the Nations, ch. 10, 11		The Singing Tree, ch. 10, 11	Across America on an Emigrant Train, ch. 5–7	The War to End All Wars, ch. 5, 6
Week 4, Lessons 76–80					
American History	Stories of America, Vol. 2, ch. 21, 22; Our Country's Presidents	(opt.) George Washington Carver, ch. 7, 8	The Wright Brothers, ch. 7, 8	The Wright Brothers: How They Invented the Airplane, ch. 9, 10	The Wright Brothers: How They Invented the Airplane, ch. 9, 10; Amer. Voices, pp. 297–302; America, Vol. 2, ch. 1
Geography	Minn of the Mississippi, ch. 6, 7, OR WorldTrek, pp. 111–120; Map Drill: United States				
Bible	2 John				
World History	Stories of the Nations, ch. 12, 13	Only a Dog, ch. 1, 2	Where Poppies Grow, pp. 4–23	World War I, ch. 1, 2	The War to End All Wars, ch. 7, 8

Week 5, Lessons 81–85				
American History	Stories of America, Vol. 2, ch. 23, 24	(opt.) George Washington Carver, ch. 9, 10	The Wright Brothers, ch. 9, 10	The Yanks Are Coming, Prelude–ch. 2	The Yanks Are Coming, Prelude–ch. 2; (American Voices, pp. 297–303)
Geography	Minn of the Mississippi, ch. 8, 9, OR WorldTrek, pp. 121–127; Map Drill: United States				
Bible	3 John				
World History	Stories of the Nations, ch. 14, 15	Only a Dog, ch. 3, 4	Where Poppies Grow, pp. 24–39	World War I, ch. 3, 4	The War to End All Wars, ch. 9, 10
Week 6, Lessons 86–90				
American History	Stories of America, Vol. 2, ch. 25 and poem	(opt.) George Washington Carver, ch. 11, 12	The Wright Brothers, ch. 11, 12	The Yanks Are Coming, ch. 3, 4	The Yanks Are Coming, ch. 3, 4
Geography	Minn of the Mississippi, ch. 10, 11, OR WorldTrek, pp. 127–133; Map Drill: United States				
Bible	Revelation study, lesson 1				
World History	Stories of the Nations, ch. 16	Only a Dog, ch. 5, 6	Where Poppies Grow, pp. 40–46	World War I, ch. 5, 6	The War to End All Wars, ch. 11, 12
Week 7, Lessons 91–95				
American History	Empire State Building	(opt.) George Washington Carver, ch. 13, 14	The Wright Brothers, ch. 13, 14	The Yanks Are Coming, ch. 5, 6	The Yanks Are Coming, ch. 5, 6
Geography	Minn of the Mississippi, ch. 12, 13, OR WorldTrek, pp. 133–139; Map Drill: United States				
Bible	Revelation study, lesson 2				
World History	Stories of the Nations, ch. 17	Only a Dog, ch. 7 and After	Snow Treasure, ch. 1–6	The Endless Steppe, ch. 1–3	The War to End All Wars, ch. 13, 14
Week 8, Lessons 96–100				
American History	Hoover Dam	(opt.) George Washington Carver, ch. 15	The Wright Brothers, ch. 15, 16	The Yanks Are Coming, ch. 7	The Yanks Are Coming, ch. 7; American Voices, pp. 305–313; America, Vol. 2, ch. 2
Geography	Minn of the Mississippi, ch. 14, 15, OR WorldTrek, pp. 139–144; Map Drill: United States				
Bible	Revelation study, lesson 3				
World History	Stories of the Nations, ch. 18, 19		Snow Treasure, ch. 7–12	The Endless Steppe, ch. 4–7	The War to End All Wars, ch. 15; Hitler, ch. 1

Week 9, Lessons 101–105				
American History	Our Country's Presidents; Stories of America, Vol. 2, ch. 26	A Boy Named FDR; Franklin and Winston	The Wright Brothers, ch. 17, 18	Victory in the Pacific, ch. 1, 2	America, Vol. 2, ch. 3, 4; American Voices, pp. 314–316
Geography	Minn of the Mississippi, ch. 16, 17, OR WorldTrek, pp. 144–150; Map Drill: United States				
Bible	Revelation study, lesson 4				
World History	Stories of the Nations, ch. 20, 21	The Little Ships; Always Remember Me	Snow Treasure, ch. 13–18	The Endless Steppe, ch. 8–13	Hitler, ch. 2, 3
Week 10, Lessons 106–110				
American History	Stories of America, Vol. 2, ch. 27, 28 and poem	Rebekkah's Journey; Lily's Victory Garden	The Wright Brothers, ch. 19, 20	Victory in the Pacific, ch. 3, 4	America, Vol. 2, ch. 5; American Voices, pp. 318, 319; Victory in the Pacific, ch. 1
Geography	Minn of the Mississippi, ch. 18, 19, OR WorldTrek, pp. 150–155; Map Drill: United States				
Bible	Revelation study, lesson 5				
World History		The Journey That Saved Curious George	Snow Treasure, ch. 19–24	The Endless Steppe, ch. 14–17	Hitler, ch. 4, 5
Week 11, Lessons 111–115				
Am. History	Stories of America, Vol. 2, ch. 29; Our Country's Presidents	The Unbreakable Code		Victory in the Pacific, ch. 5, 6	Victory in the Pacific, ch. 2, 3
Geography	Minn of the Mississippi, ch. 20, OR WorldTrek, pp. 156–161; Map Drill: United States				
Bible	Revelation study, lesson 6				
World History	Stories of the Nations, ch. 22, 23		Snow Treasure, ch. 25–30	The Endless Steppe, ch. 18–22	Hitler, ch. 6, 7
Week 12, Lessons 116–120				
Am. History	Exam or Project				Victory in the Pacific, ch. 4–6
Geography	Exam				
Bible	Exam				
World History	Exam				

Lesson 61: The Wright Brothers

Materials Needed
- *Stories of America, Vol. 2*
- (optional) *George Washington Carver* (grades 1–3)
- *The Wright Brothers: Pioneers of American Aviation* (grades 4–6)
- *The Wright Brothers: How They Invented the Airplane* (grades 7–12)

Family: Write the name "Wright Brothers" on a small whiteboard or sheet of paper so younger students can see that it begins with a *W*. Explain that these two brothers made history while Theodore Roosevelt was president. Read together *Stories of America, Volume 2*, chapter 16, "The Wright Brothers," and ask for an oral narration.

Grades 1–3: If desired, read together with your younger children *George Washington Carver*, chapter 1, "Death in the Trees, and ask for an oral narration.

Tip: This biography on Carver is completely appropriate for younger children, but the chapters may be too long for some younger students in addition to the Family reading. Use your discretion whether to include it in your studies.

Grades 4–6: Read with your older children or assign as independent reading *The Wright Brothers: Pioneers of American Aviation,* chapter 1, "Learning from Mother." Ask for an oral or written narration.

Grades 7–12: Read with your older children or assign as independent reading *The Wright Brothers: How They Invented the Airplane,* chapters 1 and 2, "What Amos Root Saw" and "Wilbur and Orville." Ask for an oral or written narration.

 # Lesson 62: Henry Ford Finds a Better Way

Materials Needed
- *Stories of America, Vol. 2*
- (optional) *George Washington Carver* (grades 1–3)
- *The Wright Brothers: Pioneers of American Aviation* (grades 4–6)
- *The Wright Brothers: How They Invented the Airplane* (grades 7–12)
- *American Voices* (grades 10–12)

Family: Ask students what they recall about the Wright Brothers. Read together *Stories of America, Volume 2*, chapter 17, "Henry Ford Finds a Better Way," and ask for an oral narration.

Grades 1–3: If desired, read together with your younger children *George*

Book of Centuries Timeline

Wright Brothers first flight (1903)

Henry Ford establishes the Ford Motor Company (1903)

Washington Carver, chapter 2, "A Quiet Voice," and ask for an oral narration.

Grades 4–6: Read with your older children or assign as independent reading *The Wright Brothers: Pioneers of American Aviation,* chapter 2, "Get It Right on Paper." Ask for an oral or written narration.

Grades 7–12: Read with your older children or assign as independent reading *The Wright Brothers: How They Invented the Airplane,* chapter 3, "The Art of Flying." Ask for an oral or written narration.

Grades 10–12: Also read with your older children or assign as independent reading *American Voices,* page 284, "This Is My Father's World."

Lesson 63: Geography Book and 1 John 3

Materials Needed
- *Minn of the Mississippi* OR *WorldTrek*
- Outline map of United States; labeled U. S. map
- Bible
- *GOAL Bible Study Journal*
- *Discovering Doctrine* (grades 7–12)

Family Geography Book: Read together *Minn of the Mississippi,* chapter 1, and ask for an oral narration OR read together *WorldTrek,* pages 92–100, and trace the Fishers' route on a map or globe.

Tip: Chapter 1 in Minn of the Mississippi *contains a paragraph of evolution. You can easily skip that fifth paragraph, beginning "This North was a land of ancient waters." Just read about the water dribbling from the "tail of a soggy crow. . . ." and skip to "The old crow had no words for talking."*

Family Map Drill: Give each student a copy of a blank outline map of the United States and encourage them to label the states on the map. Compare their labeled states with a labeled United States map and make any necessary corrections. Then have them label one or two more states on their maps, copying the spelling and locations from the labeled United States map.

Optional Extra Challenge: Make copies of page 145 in this book that lists the fifty states' two-letter abbreviations. Give each student a copy of the abbreviation list and have him write the state's name correctly next to its abbreviation. For convenience, students can use the two-letter abbreviation when labeling the map if desired. Make this optional challenge a corresponding part of the usual map drill; students can list and label the states they know, then add one or two more each week.

Family Bible Study: Read together 1 John 3, looking for any descriptions of promises, commands, sins, or principles, as explained in your *GOAL Bible Study Journal*. Record your findings in your *GOAL Bible Study Journal*.

Tip: Older students should also be listening for doctrinal truths that they can add to their ongoing Discovering Doctrine *books.*

 Lesson 64: The Boer War

Materials Needed
- *Stories of the Nations, Vol. 2*
- *The Singing Tree* (grades 4–6)
- *Across America on an Emigrant Train* (grades 7–9)
- *The War to End All Wars* (grades 10–12)

Family: Locate South Africa on the world map in the back of *Stories of the Nations, Volume 2*. Explain that today's story is about events in Africa. Read together *Stories of the Nations, Volume 2*, chapter 6, "The Boer War." Ask for an oral narration.

Grades 4–6: Read with your older children or assign as independent reading *The Singing Tree*, chapter 6, "Corporal Nagy."

Grades 7–9: Read with your older children or assign as independent reading *Across America on an Emigrant Train*, Introduction and chapter 1, "The Journey Begins." Ask for an oral or written narration.

Grades 10–12: Read with your older children or assign as independent reading *The War to End All Wars*, chapter 1, "Murder in Sarajevo." Ask for an oral or written narration.

Tip: Unfortunately, most books dealing with modern history include some swearing when quoting from direct sources. Though such quotations are not frequent in this book, you may want to warn your students to be prepared for it.

 Lesson 65: Discoveries in the Sea of Ice

Materials Needed
- *Stories of the Nations, Vol. 2*
- *The Singing Tree* (grades 4–6)
- *Across America on an Emigrant Train* (grades 7–9)
- *The War to End All Wars* (grades 10–12)

Family: Ask students what they recall about the Boer War in South Africa.

Book of Centuries Timeline

Boer War in which Great Britain defeats the Boers and claims South Africa (1899–1902)

Book of Centuries
Timeline

Peary reaches the North Pole (1909)

Discuss the various places that people had explored throughout the world by this time in history. Read together *Stories of the Nations, Volume 2,* chapter 7, "Discoveries in the Sea of Ice." Ask for an oral narration.

Grades 4–6: Read with your older children or assign as independent reading *The Singing Tree,* chapter 7, "Six Big Russians."

Grades 7–9: Read with your older children or assign as independent reading *Across America on an Emigrant Train,* chapter 2, "All Aboard!" Ask for an oral or written narration.

Grades 10–12: Read with your older children or assign as independent reading *The War to End All Wars,* chapter 2, "Armed to the Teeth." Ask for an oral or written narration.

 Lesson 66: The San Francisco Earthquake of 1906

Materials Needed
  • *Stories of America, Vol. 2*
  • (optional) *George Washington Carver* (grades 1–3)
  • *The Wright Brothers: Pioneers of American Aviation* (grades 4–6)
  • *The Wright Brothers: How They Invented the Airplane* (grades 7–12)

San Francisco earthquake (1906)

Family: Ask students what they recall about Henry Ford. Explain that while he was working peacefully in his shop, residents out west in California experienced a terrible surprise one day. Read together *Stories of America, Volume 2,* chapter 18, "The San Francisco Earthquake of 1906," and ask for an oral narration.

Grades 1–3: If desired, read together with your younger children *George Washington Carver,* chapter 3, "Off to Neosho," and ask for an oral narration.

Grades 4–6: Read with your older children or assign as independent reading *The Wright Brothers: Pioneers of American Aviation,* chapter 3, "Building a Wagon." Ask for an oral or written narration.

Grades 7–12: Read with your older children or assign as independent reading *The Wright Brothers: How They Invented the Airplane,* chapter 4, "Wind and Sand." Ask for an oral or written narration.

Lesson 67: Ellis Island

Materials Needed
  • *Stories of America, Vol. 2*
  • (optional) *George Washington Carver* (grades 1–3)

- *The Wright Brothers: Pioneers of American Aviation* (grades 4–6)
- *The Wright Brothers: How They Invented the Airplane* (grades 7–12)

Family: Ask students what they recall about the San Francisco earthquake of 1906. Explain that even that disaster did not slow the flood of people coming to America from other countries. Discuss why people might leave their homeland and what challenges America might face as all those people arrived. Read together *Stories of America, Volume 2*, chapter 19, "Ellis Island," and ask for an oral narration.

Grades 1–3: If desired, read together with your younger children *George Washington Carver*, chapter 4, "A New Home," and ask for an oral narration.

Grades 4–6: Read with your older children or assign as independent reading *The Wright Brothers: Pioneers of American Aviation*, chapter 4, "Their First Pocket Money." Ask for an oral or written narration.

Grades 7–12: Read with your older children or assign as independent reading *The Wright Brothers: How They Invented the Airplane*, chapter 5, "Back to the Drawing Board." Ask for an oral or written narration.

Ellis Island processes immigrants to U. S. (1892–1954)

Tip: Make sure older children are up to date with their Book of Centuries entries.

Reminder: Get the book America: The Last Best Hope, Volume 2, *for grades 10–12 for lesson 77. Also get* The Yanks Are Coming *for grades 7–12 for lesson 81.*

 # Lesson 68: Geography Book and 1 John 4

Materials Needed
- *Minn of the Mississippi* OR *WorldTrek*
- Outline map of United States; labeled U. S. map
- Bible
- *GOAL Bible Study Journal*
- *Discovering Doctrine* (grades 7–12)

Family Geography Book: Ask students what they recall from last time's reading about the turtle eggs. Read together *Minn of the Mississippi*, chapters 2 and 3, and ask for an oral narration OR read together *WorldTrek*, pages 100–104, and trace the Fishers' route on a map or globe.

Family Map Drill: Give each student a copy of a blank outline map of the United States and encourage them to label the states on the map. Include the optional state abbreviations challenge if desired. Compare their labeled states with a labeled United States map and make any necessary

Book of Centuries Timeline

Tesla, Marconi, and Landell work to create radio (1891–1901)

corrections. Then have them label one or two more states on their maps, copying the spelling and locations from the labeled United States map.

Family Bible Study: Read together 1 John 4, looking for any descriptions of promises, commands, sins, or principles, as explained in your *GOAL Bible Study Journal*. Record your findings in your *GOAL Bible Study Journal*.

Tip: Older students should also be listening for doctrinal truths that they can add to their ongoing Discovering Doctrine *books.*

 # Lesson 69: Waves around the World

Materials Needed
- *Stories of the Nations, Vol. 2*
- *The Singing Tree* (grades 4–6)
- *Across America on an Emigrant Train* (grades 7–9)
- *The War to End All Wars* (grades 10–12)

Family: Ask students what they recall about the quest to reach the North Pole. Explain that other men at the time were focused on different quests, not of exploration but of inventions. Read together *Stories of the Nations, Volume 2*, chapter 8, "Waves around the World." Ask for an oral narration.

Grades 4–6: Read with your older children or assign as independent reading *The Singing Tree,* chapter 8, "Just Came."

Grades 7–9: Read with your older children or assign as independent reading *Across America on an Emigrant Train,* chapter 3, "Aboard the Emigrant Train." Ask for an oral or written narration.

Grades 10–12: Read with your older children or assign as independent reading *The War to End All Wars,* chapter 3, "To Berlin! To Paris!" Ask for an oral or written narration.

Reminder: Get the books Only a Dog *for grades 1–3,* Where Poppies Grow *for grades 4–6, and* World War I *for grades 7–9 for lesson 79.*

 # Lesson 70: The Prizes of Alfred Nobel

Materials Needed
- *Stories of the Nations, Vol. 2*
- *The Singing Tree* (grades 4–6)
- *Across America on an Emigrant Train* (grades 7–9)
- *The War to End All Wars* (grades 10–12)

Family: Ask students what they recall about the story of radio. Help students find Sweden on the world map in the back of *Stories of the Nations, Volume 2,* or on a globe. Explain that today's story starts in Sweden. Read together *Stories of the Nations, Volume 2,* chapter 9, "The Prizes of Alfred Nobel." Ask for an oral narration.

Grades 4–6: Read with your older children or assign as independent reading *The Singing Tree,* chapter 9, "Light a Candle."

Grades 7–9: Read with your older children or assign as independent reading *Across America on an Emigrant Train,* chapter 4, "Into the Wild West." Ask for an oral or written narration.

Grades 10–12: Read with your older children or assign as independent reading *The War to End All Wars,* chapter 4, "The Most Terrible August in the History of the World." Ask for an oral or written narration.

Book of Centuries Timeline

Alfred Nobel invents dynamite (1867)

First Nobel Peace prizes awarded (1901)

Lesson 71: The Fire That Changed America

Materials Needed
- *Stories of America, Vol. 2*
- (optional) *George Washington Carver* (grades 1–3)
- *The Wright Brothers: Pioneers of American Aviation* (grades 4–6)
- *The Wright Brothers: How They Invented the Airplane* (grades 7–12)
- *American Voices* (grades 10–12)

Family: Ask students what they recall about immigrants and Ellis Island. Discuss what kinds of jobs the arriving immigrants might look for as they began their new lives in America. Read together *Stories of America, Volume 2,* chapter 20, "The Fire That Changed America," and ask for an oral narration.

Triangle Shirtwaist Factory fire prompts changes to working conditions (1911)

Grades 1–3: If desired, read together with your younger children *George Washington Carver,* chapter 5, "Journey to Nowhere," and ask for an oral narration.

Grades 4–6: Read with your older children or assign as independent reading *The Wright Brothers: Pioneers of American Aviation,* chapter 5, "Making Kites." Ask for an oral or written narration.

Grades 7–12: Read with your older children or assign as independent reading *The Wright Brothers: How They Invented the Airplane,* chapter 6, "Horsepower and Propellers." Ask for an oral or written narration.

Grades 10–12: Also read with your older children or assign as independent reading *American Voices,* selected hymns on pages 294–296.

Lesson 72: A Nation's Strength

Materials Needed
- *Stories of America, Vol. 2*
- (optional) *George Washington Carver* (grades 1–3)
- *The Wright Brothers: Pioneers of American Aviation* (grades 4–6)
- *The Wright Brothers: How They Invented the Airplane* (grades 7–12)

Family: Read together the poem "A Nation's Strength" on page 127 of *Stories of America, Volume 2*. Ask the children if they have read this year about any men like this poem describes. Encourage them to share their thoughts and narrations about men who stand fast and suffer long for truth and honor, who work while others sleep, and who dare while others fly.

Grades 1–3: If desired, read together with your younger children *George Washington Carver*, chapter 6, "Caught in a Blizzard," and ask for an oral narration.

Grades 4–6: Read with your older children or assign as independent reading *The Wright Brothers: Pioneers of American Aviation*, chapter 6, "Wilbur's Illness." Ask for an oral or written narration.

Grades 7–12: Read with your older children or assign as independent reading *The Wright Brothers: How They Invented the Airplane*, chapters 7 and 8, "The First Practical Airplane" and "Fliers or Liars?" Ask for an oral or written narration.

Lesson 73: Geography Book and 1 John 5

Materials Needed
- *Minn of the Mississippi* OR *WorldTrek*
- Outline map of United States; labeled U. S. map
- Bible
- *GOAL Bible Study Journal*
- *Discovering Doctrine* (grades 7–12)

Family Geography Book: Ask students what they recall from last time's reading about Minn and his first days. Read together *Minn of the Mississippi*, chapters 4 and 5, and ask for an oral narration OR read together *WorldTrek*, pages 104–111, and trace the Fishers' route on a map or globe.

Tip: Chapter 4 in Minn of the Mississippi *contains a reference to evolution at the end of the chapter. You can skip it by stopping the reading at "made a picnic of sending Minn down the River," or you can read the whole chapter and discuss that last section with the children.*

Tip: Be sure to pay attention to the little maps in the margins of certain pages as you work your way through Minn of the Mississippi. *If you have several students trying to see the map, you may want to trace Minn's route on a larger map of the Mississippi River region.*

Family Map Drill: Give each student a copy of a blank outline map of the United States and encourage them to label the states on the map. Include the optional state abbreviations challenge if desired. Compare their labeled states with a labeled United States map and make any necessary corrections. Then have them label one or two more states on their maps, copying the spelling and locations from the labeled United States map.

Family Bible Study: Read together 1 John 5, looking for any descriptions of promises, commands, sins, or principles, as explained in your *GOAL Bible Study Journal*. Record your findings in your *GOAL Bible Study Journal*.

Tip: Older students should also be listening for doctrinal truths that they can add to their ongoing Discovering Doctrine *books.*

Lesson 74: Marie Curie

Materials Needed
- *Stories of the Nations, Vol. 2*
- *The Singing Tree* (grades 4–6)
- *Across America on an Emigrant Train* (grades 7–9)
- *The War to End All Wars* (grades 10–12)

Family: Ask students what they recall about Alfred Nobel and his prizes. Help students locate Poland—where today's story begins—on the world map or a globe. Read together *Stories of the Nations, Volume 2*, chapter 10, "Marie Curie." Ask for an oral narration.

Grades 4–6: Read with your older children or assign as independent reading *The Singing Tree*, chapter 10, "Six Little Germans."

Grades 7–9: Read with your older children or assign as independent reading *Across America on an Emigrant Train*, chapter 5, "Across the High Sierras." Ask for an oral or written narration.

Grades 10–12: Read with your older children or assign as independent reading *The War to End All Wars*, chapter 5, "Stalemate." Ask for an oral or written narration.

Lesson 75: On a Beam of Light

Materials Needed
- *Stories of the Nations, Vol. 2*

Book of Centuries Timeline

Marie and Pierre Curie discover radium and work with radioactivity (1903 Nobel prize)

**Book of Centuries
Timeline**

*Albert Einstein's Theory of Relativity
(1917)*

• *The Singing Tree* (grades 4–6)
• *Across America on an Emigrant Train* (grades 7–9)
• *The War to End All Wars* (grades 10–12)

Family: Ask students what they recall about Marie Curie. Explain that today's story is about another scientist, a physicist who lived in Switzerland. Find Switzerland on a world map or globe, then read together *Stories of the Nations, Volume 2*, chapter 11, "On a Beam of Light." Ask for an oral narration.

Grades 4–6: Read with your older children or assign as independent reading *The Singing Tree,* chapter 11, "The Singing Tree."

Grades 7–9: Read with your older children or assign as independent reading *Across America on an Emigrant Train,* chapters 6 and 7, "In the Good Country" and "A Final Word." Ask for an oral or written narration.

Grades 10–12: Read with your older children or assign as independent reading *The War to End All Wars,* chapter 6, "The Technology of Death and Destruction." Ask for an oral or written narration.

 # Lesson 76: The Sinking of the *Titanic*

Materials Needed
• *Stories of America, Vol. 2*
• (optional) *George Washington Carver* (grades 1–3)
• *The Wright Brothers: Pioneers of American Aviation* (grades 4–6)
• *The Wright Brothers: How They Invented the Airplane* (grades 7–12)

*The "unsinkable" Titanic sinks
(1912)*

Family: Read together *Stories of America, Volume 2,* chapter 21, "The Great Tragedy of 1912: The Sinking of the *Titanic.*" Ask for an oral narration.

Grades 1–3: If desired, read together with your younger children *George Washington Carver*, chapter 7, "Magic Hands," and ask for an oral narration.

Grades 4–6: Read with your older children or assign as independent reading *The Wright Brothers: Pioneers of American Aviation,* chapter 7, "The Helicopter." Ask for an oral or written narration.

Grades 7–12: Read with your older children or assign as independent reading *The Wright Brothers: How They Invented the Airplane,* chapters 9 and 10, "The Conquering Heroes" and "The Age of Flight." Ask for an oral or written narration.

 # Lesson 77: The War to End All Wars

Materials Needed
• *Stories of America, Vol. 2*

- *Our Country's Presidents*
- (optional) *George Washington Carver* (grades 1–3)
- *The Wright Brothers: Pioneers of American Aviation* (grades 4–6)
- *America: The Last Best Hope, Vol. 2* (grades 10–12)
- *American Voices* (grades 10–12)

Family: Ask students what they recall about the sinking of the *Titanic*. Read together *Stories of America, Volume 2,* chapter 22, "The War to End All Wars." Ask for an oral narration.

Look together at *Our Country's Presidents,* the section on Woodrow Wilson.

World War I (1914–1918)

Grades 1–3: If desired, read together with your younger children *George Washington Carver,* chapter 8, "Surprise Meeting," and ask for an oral narration.

Grades 4–6: Read with your older children or assign as independent reading *The Wright Brothers: Pioneers of American Aviation,* chapter 8, "The West Side *Tatler.*" Ask for an oral or written narration.

Grades 10–12: Read with your older children or assign as independent reading *America: The Last Best Hope, Volume 2,* chapter 1, "America and the Great War." Ask for an oral or written narration.

Also read with your older children or assign as independent reading *American Voices,* pages 297–302, Woodrow Wilson's "War Message to Congress." Students may read only part of the speech today and finish it on your next American History study day if desired.

Tip: Make sure older children are up to date with their Book of Centuries entries.

Lesson 78: Geography Book and 2 John

Materials Needed
- *Minn of the Mississippi* OR *WorldTrek*
- Outline map of United States; labeled U. S. map
- Bible
- *GOAL Bible Study Journal*
- *Discovering Doctrine* (grades 7–12)

Family Geography Book: Ask students what they recall from last time's reading about Minn's survival and egg-laying. Read together *Minn of the Mississippi,* chapters 6 and 7, and ask for an oral narration OR read together *WorldTrek,* pages 111–120, and trace the Fishers' route on a map or globe.

Family Map Drill: Give each student a copy of a blank outline map of the

TERM

Book of Centuries Timeline

United States and encourage them to label the states on the map. Include the optional state abbreviations challenge if desired. Compare their labeled states with a labeled United States map and make any necessary corrections. Then have them label one or two more states on their maps, copying the spelling and locations from the labeled United States map.

Family Bible Study: Read together 2 John, looking for any descriptions of promises, commands, sins, or principles, as explained in your *GOAL Bible Study Journal*. Record your findings in your *GOAL Bible Study Journal*.

Tip: Older students should also be listening for doctrinal truths that they can add to their ongoing Discovering Doctrine *books.*

Reminder: Get the book Come, Lord Jesus: Lessons from Revelation *for Family Bible study for lesson 88.*

 # Lesson 79: The War to End All Wars

Materials Needed
- *Stories of the Nations, Vol. 2*
- *Only a Dog* (grades 1–3)
- *Where Poppies Grow* (grades 4–6)
- *World War I: From the Lusitania to Versailles* (grades 7–9)
- *The War to End All Wars* (grades 10–12)

Family: Ask students what they recall about Albert Einstein and his work. Read together *Stories of the Nations, Volume 2*, chapter 12, "The War to End All Wars." Use the map "Europe before World War I, 1914" in the back of *Stories of the Nations, Volume 2*, as you read about the various countries' roles in the war. Ask for an oral narration.

Grades 1–3: Read with your younger children *Only a Dog*, chapter 1.

Grades 4–6: Read with your older children or assign as independent reading *Where Poppies Grow*, pages 4–13, from "War!" to "The Routine of Daily Life." Ask for an oral or written narration.

Grades 7–9: Read with your older children or assign as independent reading *World War I: From the Lusitania to Versailles*, chapter 1, "The Sinking of the Lusitania." Ask for an oral or written narration.

Tip: Unfortunately, most books dealing with modern history include some swearing when quoting from direct sources. Though such quotations are not frequent in this book (We noticed three.), you may want to warn your students to be prepared for it.

Grades 10–12: Read with your older children or assign as independent

reading *The War to End All Wars,* chapter 7, "Life and Death in the Trenches." Ask for an oral or written narration.

 # Lesson 80: The Christmas Truce

Materials Needed
- *Stories of the Nations, Vol. 2*
- *Only a Dog* (grades 1–3)
- *Where Poppies Grow* (grades 4–6)
- *World War I: From the Lusitania to Versailles* (grades 7–9)
- *The War to End All Wars* (grades 10–12)

Family: Ask students what they recall about how World War I started. Read together *Stories of the Nations, Volume 2,* chapter 13, "The Christmas Truce." Ask for an oral narration.

Grades 1–3: Read with your younger children *Only a Dog,* chapter 2.

Grades 4–6: Read with your older children or assign as independent reading *Where Poppies Grow,* pages 14–23, from "Over the Top" to "You Have Suffered Terribly." Ask for an oral or written narration.

Grades 7–9: Read with your older children or assign as independent reading *World War I: From the Lusitania to Versailles,* chapter 2, "The World at War." Ask for an oral or written narration.

Grades 10–12: Read with your older children or assign as independent reading *The War to End All Wars,* chapter 8, "Over the Top." Ask for an oral or written narration.

 # Lesson 81: On the Home Front

Materials Needed
- *Stories of America, Vol. 2*
- (optional) *George Washington Carver* (grades 1–3)
- *The Wright Brothers: Pioneers of American Aviation* (grades 4–6)
- *The Yanks Are Coming* (grades 7–12)
- *American Voices* (grades 10–12)

Family: Ask students what they recall about World War I. Make sure they understand that the countries in Europe were fighting for several years before America sent over our own soldiers. Read together *Stories of America, Volume 2,* chapter 23, "On the Home Front: Doing Our Bit During World War I." Ask for an oral narration.

Grades 1–3: If desired, read together with your younger children *George*

Washington Carver, chapter 9, "A Plea for Help," and ask for an oral narration.

Grades 4–6: Read with your older children or assign as independent reading *The Wright Brothers: Pioneers of American Aviation*, chapter 9, "The Wright Cycle Company." Ask for an oral or written narration.

Grades 7–12: Read with your older children or assign as independent reading *The Yanks Are Coming*, "Prelude: The Passing of a Sea Queen," and chapter 1, "War Comes to America." Ask for an oral or written narration.

Grades 10–12: Also read with your older children or assign as independent reading *American Voices*, the rest of Woodrow Wilson's "War Message to Congress" on pages 297–302, if needed.

Reminder: Get the books Empire State Building *and* Hoover Dam *for Family for lessons 91 and 96.*

 ## Lesson 82: Corporal York Defeats the Machine Gun

Materials Needed
- *Stories of America, Vol. 2*
- (optional) *George Washington Carver* (grades 1–3)
- *The Wright Brothers: Pioneers of American Aviation* (grades 4–6)
- *The Yanks Are Coming* (grades 7–12)
- *American Voices* (grades 10–12)

Family: Ask students what they recall about World War I and ways America played a role in it. Read together *Stories of America, Volume 2*, chapter 24, "Corporal York Defeats the Machine Gun." Ask for an oral narration.

Grades 1–3: If desired, read together with your younger children *George Washington Carver*, chapter 10, "Strange Treasure," and ask for an oral narration.

Grades 4–6: Read with your older children or assign as independent reading *The Wright Brothers: Pioneers of American Aviation*, chapter 10, "The Bicycle Race." Ask for an oral or written narration.

Grades 7–12: Read with your older children or assign as independent reading *The Yanks Are Coming*, chapter 2, "Crossing the Big Pond." Ask for an oral or written narration.

Grades 10–12: Also read with your older children or assign as independent reading *American Voices*, page 303, the lyrics to "Over There."

Lesson 83: Geography Book and 3 John

Materials Needed
- *Minn of the Mississippi* OR *WorldTrek*
- Outline map of United States; labeled U. S. map
- Bible
- *GOAL Bible Study Journal*
- *Discovering Doctrine* (grades 7–12)

Family Geography Book: Ask students what they recall from last time's reading about the museum in the river and the water-wall. Read together *Minn of the Mississippi*, chapters 8 and 9, and ask for an oral narration OR read together *WorldTrek*, pages 121–127, and trace the Fishers' route on a map or globe.

Family Map Drill: Give each student a copy of a blank outline map of the United States and encourage them to label the states on the map. Include the optional state abbreviations challenge if desired. Compare their labeled states with a labeled United States map and make any necessary corrections. Then have them label one or two more states on their maps, copying the spelling and locations from the labeled United States map.

Family Bible Study: Read together 3 John, looking for any descriptions of promises, commands, sins, or principles, as explained in your *GOAL Bible Study Journal*. Record your findings in your *GOAL Bible Study Journal*.

Tip: Older students should also be listening for doctrinal truths that they can add to their ongoing Discovering Doctrine *books.*

 # Lesson 84: The Red Baron

Materials Needed
- *Stories of the Nations, Vol. 2*
- *Only a Dog* (grades 1–3)
- *Where Poppies Grow* (grades 4–6)
- *World War I: From the Lusitania to Versailles* (grades 7–9)
- *The War to End All Wars* (grades 10–12)

Family: Ask students what they recall about the Christmas truce during World War I. Discuss with the students what a hero is and whether they would consider any of the men in that story to be a hero. Read together *Stories of the Nations, Volume 2*, chapter 14, "The Red Baron." Ask for an oral narration.

Grades 1–3: Read with your younger children *Only a Dog*, chapter 3.

Grades 4–6: Read with your older children or assign as independent reading *Where Poppies Grow*, pages 24–33, from "Propaganda & Patriotism" to "The Poppy Poem." Ask for an oral or written narration.

Grades 7–9: Read with your older children or assign as independent reading *World War I: From the Lusitania to Versailles*, chapter 3, "The Yanks Are Coming." Ask for an oral or written narration.

Grades 10–12: Read with your older children or assign as independent reading *The War to End All Wars*, chapter 9, "The Battle of Verdun." Ask for an oral or written narration.

Reminder: Get the books Snow Treasure *for grades 4–6 and* The Endless Steppe *for grades 7–9 for lesson 94.*

Lesson 85: The Last Journey of the *Lusitania*

Materials Needed
- *Stories of the Nations, Vol. 2*
- *Only a Dog* (grades 1–3)
- *Where Poppies Grow* (grades 4–6)
- *World War I: From the Lusitania to Versailles* (grades 7–9)
- *The War to End All Wars* (grades 10–12)

Family: Ask students what they recall about the Red Baron. Explain that today's story turns from the skies down to the sea. Read together *Stories of the Nations, Volume 2*, chapter 15, "The Last Journey of the *Lusitania*." Ask for an oral narration.

Grades 1–3: Read with your younger children *Only a Dog*, chapter 4.

Grades 4–6: Read with your older children or assign as independent reading *Where Poppies Grow*, pages 34–39, from "Angels, Statues, & Songs in the Night" to "Man's Best Friend." Ask for an oral or written narration.

Grades 7–9: Read with your older children or assign as independent reading *World War I: From the Lusitania to Versailles*, chapter 4, "Rendezvous With Death." Ask for an oral or written narration.

Grades 10–12: Read with your older children or assign as independent reading *The War to End All Wars*, chapter 10, "The Battle of the Somme." Ask for an oral or written narration.

Lesson 86: America the Beautiful

Materials Needed
- *Stories of America, Vol. 2*

- (optional) *George Washington Carver* (grades 1–3)
- *The Wright Brothers: Pioneers of American Aviation* (grades 4–6)
- *The Yanks Are Coming* (grades 7–12)

Family: Ask students what they recall about the end of World War I. Read together the poem "America the Beautiful" from *Stories of America, Volume 2,* page 153. Ask students to listen for phrases that might describe what people were thinking and feeling during the war.

Grades 1–3: If desired, read together with your younger children *George Washington Carver,* chapter 11, "Secrets of the Soil," and ask for an oral narration.

Grades 4–6: Read with your older children or assign as independent reading *The Wright Brothers: Pioneers of American Aviation,* chapter 11, "In the Bicycle Business." Ask for an oral or written narration.

Grades 7–12: Read with your older children or assign as independent reading *The Yanks Are Coming,* chapter 3, "Lafayette, We Are Here!" Ask for an oral or written narration.

Lesson 87: A Roar and a Crash

Materials Needed
- *Stories of America, Vol. 2*
- *Our Country's Presidents*
- (optional) *George Washington Carver* (grades 1–3)
- *The Wright Brothers: Pioneers of American Aviation* (grades 4–6)
- *The Yanks Are Coming* (grades 7–12)

U. S. stock market crashes (1929)

Family: Read together *Stories of America, Volume 2,* chapter 25, "A Roar and a Crash." Ask for an oral narration.

Look together at *Our Country's Presidents,* the section on Herbert Hoover.

Grades 1–3: If desired, read together with your younger children *George Washington Carver,* chapter 12, "School on Wheels," and ask for an oral narration.

Grades 4–6: Read with your older children or assign as independent reading *The Wright Brothers: Pioneers of American Aviation,* chapter 12, "Typhoid Fever." Ask for an oral or written narration.

Grades 7–12: Read with your older children or assign as independent reading *The Yanks Are Coming,* chapter 4, "Trial by Fire." Ask for an oral or written narration.

Tip: Make sure older children are up to date with their Book of Centuries entries.

Lesson 88: Geography Book and Revelation 1

Materials Needed
- *Minn of the Mississippi* OR *WorldTrek*
- Outline map of United States; labeled U. S. map
- Bible
- *Come, Lord Jesus: Lessons from Revelation*
- *Discovering Doctrine* (grades 7–12)

Family Geography Book: Ask students what they recall from last time's reading about Minn as a river-monster and the lake in the river. Read together *Minn of the Mississippi*, chapters 10 and 11, and ask for an oral narration OR read together *WorldTrek*, pages 127–133, and trace the Fishers' route on a map or globe.

Family Map Drill: Give each student a copy of a blank outline map of the United States and encourage them to label the states on the map. Include the optional state abbreviations challenge if desired. Compare their labeled states with a labeled United States map and make any necessary corrections. Then have them label one or two more states on their maps, copying the spelling and locations from the labeled United States map.

Family Bible Study: Complete *Come, Lord Jesus: Lessons from Revelation*, lesson 1.

Tip: Older students should also be listening for doctrinal truths that they can add to their ongoing Discovering Doctrine *books.*

Lesson 89: World War I continued

Materials Needed
- *Only a Dog* (grades 1–3)
- *Where Poppies Grow* (grades 4–6)
- *World War I: From the Lusitania to Versailles* (grades 7–9)
- *The War to End All Wars* (grades 10–12)

Grades 1–3: Read with your younger children *Only a Dog*, chapter 5.

Grades 4–6: Read with your older children or assign as independent reading *Where Poppies Grow,* pages 40–46, from "Dear Cora" to "In Solemn Tribute." Ask for an oral or written narration.

Grades 7–9: Read with your older children or assign as independent reading *World War I: From the Lusitania to Versailles,* chapter 5, "The Eleventh Hour." Ask for an oral or written narration.

Grades 10–12: Read with your older children or assign as independent reading *The War to End All Wars,* chapter 11, "The War at Sea." Ask for an oral or written narration.

 # Lesson 90: The Russian Revolution

Materials Needed
- *Stories of the Nations, Vol. 2*
- *Only a Dog* (grades 1–3)
- *World War I: From the Lusitania to Versailles* (grades 7–9)
- *The War to End All Wars* (grades 10–12)

Family: Discuss what different factors can start a war. Is a war the same as a revolution? What is a revolution? Explain that in the midst of World War I, one of the countries also experienced a revolution. Read together *Stories of the Nations, Volume 2*, chapter 16, "The Russian Revolution." Ask for an oral narration.

Grades 1–3: Read with your younger children *Only a Dog*, chapter 6.

Grades 7–9: Read with your older children or assign as independent reading *World War I: From the Lusitania to Versailles,* chapter 6, "The Aftermath." Ask for an oral or written narration.

Grades 10–12: Read with your older children or assign as independent reading *The War to End All Wars,* chapter 12, "Mutiny, Revolution, and the Collapse of Armies." Ask for an oral or written narration.

Reminder: Get the book Hitler *for grades 10–12 for lesson 100.*

 # Lesson 91: Empire State Building, part 1

Materials Needed
- *Empire State Building*
- (optional) *George Washington Carver* (grades 1–3)
- *The Wright Brothers: Pioneers of American Aviation* (grades 4–6)
- *The Yanks Are Coming* (grades 7–12)

Family: Ask students what they recall about the Roaring Twenties and the Great Depression. Explain that not everyone lost all their money when the stock market crashed. Today they will start reading about a huge, expensive project that two men thought of and financed during that time. Read together *Empire State Building*, pages 4–23, and ask for an oral narration.

Grades 1–3: If desired, read together with your younger children *George*

Book of Centuries Timeline

Russian Revolution leads to Soviet Union (1917)

Ford Motor Company produces 10 millionth car (1924)

2.5 million radios in use in U. S. (1924)

Empire State Building erected in New York (1930–1931)

Book of Centuries Timeline

Washington Carver, chapter 13, "Fighting a Killer," and ask for an oral narration.

Grades 4–6: Read with your older children or assign as independent reading *The Wright Brothers: Pioneers of American Aviation*, chapter 13, "Learning Through Reading." Ask for an oral or written narration.

Grades 7–12: Read with your older children or assign as independent reading *The Yanks Are Coming,* chapter 5, "The Home Front." Ask for an oral or written narration.

Reminder: Get the books A Boy Named FDR, Franklin and Winston, Rebekkah's Journey, Lily's Victory Garden, *and* The Unbreakable Code *for grades 1–3 for lessons 101, 102, 106, 107, and 111. Also get* Victory in the Pacific *for grades 7–12 for lesson 101 or 107.*

 # Lesson 92: Empire State Building, part 2

Materials Needed
- *Empire State Building*
- (optional) *George Washington Carver* (grades 1–3)
- *The Wright Brothers: Pioneers of American Aviation* (grades 4–6)
- *The Yanks Are Coming* (grades 7–12)

Family: Ask students what they recall so far about the Empire State Building project. Read together *Empire State Building*, pages 24–45, and ask for an oral narration.

Grades 1–3: If desired, read together with your younger children *George Washington Carver*, chapter 14, "Big Decisions," and ask for an oral narration.

Grades 4–6: Read with your older children or assign as independent reading *The Wright Brothers: Pioneers of American Aviation,* chapter 14, "They Make a Glider." Ask for an oral or written narration.

Grades 7–12: Read with your older children or assign as independent reading *The Yanks Are Coming,* chapter 6, "Aces High." Ask for an oral or written narration.

 # Lesson 93: Geography Book and Revelation 2

Materials Needed
- *Minn of the Mississippi* OR *WorldTrek*
- Outline map of United States; labeled U. S. map
- Bible
- *Come, Lord Jesus: Lessons from Revelation*

• *Discovering Doctrine* (grades 7–12)

Family Geography Book: Ask students what they recall from last time's reading about the history of the towns' names and the many dams Minn encountered. Read together *Minn of the Mississippi*, chapters 12 and 13, and ask for an oral narration OR read together *WorldTrek*, pages 133–139, and trace the Fishers' route on a map or globe.

Family Map Drill: Give each student a copy of a blank outline map of the United States and encourage them to label the states on the map. Include the optional state abbreviations challenge if desired. Compare their labeled states with a labeled United States map and make any necessary corrections. Then have them label one or two more states on their maps, copying the spelling and locations from the labeled United States map.

Family Bible Study: Complete *Come, Lord Jesus: Lessons from Revelation*, lesson 2.

Tip: Older students should also be listening for doctrinal truths that they can add to their ongoing Discovering Doctrine *books.*

Lesson 94: Between the Wars

Materials Needed
• *Only a Dog* (grades 1–3)
• *Snow Treasure* (grades 4–6)
• *The Endless Steppe* (grades 7–9)
• *The War to End All Wars* (grades 10–12)

Grades 1–3: Read with your younger children *Only a Dog*, chapter 7.

Grades 4–6: Read with your older children or assign as independent reading *Snow Treasure*, chapters 1–3.

Tip: Snow Treasure is a wonderful tale of adventure that would be completely appropriate for grades 1–3 also, if your younger children want to listen in.

Grades 7–9: Read with your older children or assign as independent reading *The Endless Steppe*, chapter 1.

Grades 10–12: Read with your older children or assign as independent reading *The War to End All Wars*, chapter 13, "Lafayette, We Are Here!" Ask for an oral or written narration.

Reminder: Get the books The Little Ships, Always Remember Me, *and* The Journey that Saved Curious George *for grades 1–3 for lessons 104, 105, 109, and 110.*

---

*Book of Centuries
Timeline*

*Great Depression in most major
countries (1930s)*

*Hoover Dam built to control the
Colorado River and irrigation
(1920–1935)*

 # Lesson 95: The Great Depression

Materials Needed
- *Stories of the Nations, Vol. 2*
- *Only a Dog* (grades 1–3)
- *Snow Treasure* (grades 4–6)
- *The Endless Steppe* (grades 7–9)
- *The War to End All Wars* (grades 10–12)

Family: Ask students what they recall about the Russian Revolution. Read together *Stories of the Nations, Volume 2*, chapter 17, "The Great Depression." Ask for an oral narration.

Grades 1–3: Read with your younger children *Only a Dog*, After.

Grades 4–6: Read with your older children or assign as independent reading *Snow Treasure,* chapters 4–6.

Grades 7–9: Read with your older children or assign as independent reading *The Endless Steppe,* chapters 2 and 3.

Grades 10–12: Read with your older children or assign as independent reading *The War to End All Wars,* chapter 14, "The Last Offensive and the Collapse of Empires." Ask for an oral or written narration.

 # Lesson 96: The Hoover Dam, part 1

Materials Needed
- *Hoover Dam*
- (optional) *George Washington Carver* (grades 1–3)
- *The Wright Brothers: Pioneers of American Aviation* (grades 4–6)
- *The Yanks Are Coming* (grades 7–12)
- *American Voices* (grades 10–12)

Family: Ask students what they recall about the Empire State Building project. Explain that the government also had a project going out West. Read together *Hoover Dam*, pages 4–23, and ask for an oral narration.

Tip: The first paragraph on page 11 refers to "millions of years of erosion." Feel free to change it to "many years" or read it as is and discuss that evolutionary statement with your children.

Grades 1–3: If desired, read together with your younger children *George Washington Carver*, chapter 15, "Twilight," and ask for an oral narration.

Grades 4–6: Read with your older children or assign as independent reading *The Wright Brothers: Pioneers of American Aviation*, chapter 15, "Kitty Hawk." Ask for an oral or written narration.

Grades 7–12: Read with your older children or assign as independent reading *The Yanks Are Coming*, chapter 7, "Breakthrough to Victory." Ask for an oral or written narration.

Grades 10–12: Also read with your older children or assign as independent reading *American Voices*, pages 305 and 306, Woodrow Wilson's "Fourteen Points Speech."

Lesson 97: The Hoover Dam, part 2

Materials Needed
- *Hoover Dam*
- *The Wright Brothers: Pioneers of American Aviation* (grades 4–6)
- *America: The Last Best Hope, Vol. 2* (grades 10–12)
- *American Voices* (grades 10–12)

Family: Ask students what they recall so far about the Hoover Dam project. Read together *Hoover Dam*, pages 24–45, and ask for an oral narration.

Tip: The first paragraph on page 32 refers to silt deposited over "millions of years." Feel free to change it to "many years" or discuss that evolutionary statement with your children.

Grades 4–6: Read with your older children or assign as independent reading *The Wright Brothers: Pioneers of American Aviation*, chapter 16, "Improving the Glider." Ask for an oral or written narration.

Grades 10–12: Read with your older children or assign as independent reading *America: The Last Best Hope, Volume 2*, chapter 2, "The Boom and the Bust." Ask for an oral or written narration.

Also read with your older children or assign as independent reading *American Voices*, pages 307–313, two poems and Calvin Coolidge's "The Destiny of America."

Tip: Make sure older children are up to date with their Book of Centuries entries.

Lesson 98: Geography Book and Revelation 3

Materials Needed
- *Minn of the Mississippi* OR *WorldTrek*
- Outline map of United States; labeled U. S. map
- Bible

• *Come, Lord Jesus: Lessons from Revelation*
• *Discovering Doctrine* (grades 7–12)

Family Geography Book: Ask students what they recall from last time's reading about Minn's time on the *Evangeline* and the Middle Mississippi. Read together *Minn of the Mississippi*, chapters 14 and 15, and ask for an oral narration OR read together *WorldTrek*, pages 139–144, and trace the Fishers' route on a map or globe.

Family Map Drill: Give each student a copy of a blank outline map of the United States and encourage them to label the states on the map. Include the optional state abbreviations challenge if desired. Compare their labeled states with a labeled United States map and make any necessary corrections. Then have them label one or two more states on their maps, copying the spelling and locations from the labeled United States map.

Family Bible Study: Complete *Come, Lord Jesus: Lessons from Revelation*, lesson 3.

Tip: Older students should also be listening for doctrinal truths that they can add to their ongoing Discovering Doctrine *books.*

Lesson 99: The *Hindenberg*

Materials Needed
• *Stories of the Nations, Vol. 2*
• *Snow Treasure* (grades 4–6)
• *The Endless Steppe* (grades 7–9)
• *The War to End All Wars* (grades 10–12)

The Hindenberg *airship explodes (1937)*

Family: Read together *Stories of the Nations, Volume 2*, chapter 18, "The *Hindenberg*." Ask for an oral narration.

Grades 4–6: Read with your older children or assign as independent reading *Snow Treasure*, chapters 7–9.

Grades 7–9: Read with your older children or assign as independent reading *The Endless Steppe,* chapters 4 and 5.

Grades 10–12: Read with your older children or assign as independent reading *The War to End All Wars,* chapter 15, "Losing the Peace." Ask for an oral or written narration.

Lesson 100: Chain Home

Materials Needed
• *Stories of the Nations, Vol. 2*

• *Snow Treasure* (grades 4–6)
• *The Endless Steppe* (grades 7–9)
• *Hitler* (grades 10–12)

Family: Ask students what they recall about the *Hindenberg*. Explain that today's story is about an invention that took more than twenty years to perfect, but it was finished just in time. Read together *Stories of the Nations, Volume 2*, chapter 19, "Chain Home." Ask for an oral narration.

Grades 4–6: Read with your older children or assign as independent reading *Snow Treasure,* chapters 10–12.

Grades 7–9: Read with your older children or assign as independent reading *The Endless Steppe,* chapters 6 and 7.

Grades 10–12: Read with your older children or assign as independent reading *Hitler,* the chapter "Young Adolf." Ask for an oral or written narration.

Robert Watson-Watts creates a protective chain of RADAR around England (1937–1939)

 # Lesson 101: Franklin Delano Roosevelt

Materials Needed
• *Our Country's Presidents*
• *A Boy Named FDR* (grades 1–3)
• *The Wright Brothers: Pioneers of American Aviation* (grades 4–6)
• *Victory in the Pacific* (grades 7–9)
• *America: The Last Best Hope, Vol. 2* (grades 10–12)
• *American Voices* (grades 10–12)

Family: Look together at *Our Country's Presidents,* the section on Franklin D. Roosevelt. For younger students, skim the photograph captions so you can explain each photo to them. Older students can read the biographical sketch for themselves.

Grades 1–3: Read with your younger children *A Boy Named FDR.*

Grades 4–6: Read with your older children or assign as independent reading *The Wright Brothers: Pioneers of American Aviation,* chapter 17, "The Wright Engine." Ask for an oral or written narration.

Grades 7–9: Read with your older children or assign as independent reading *Victory in the Pacific,* chapter 1, "Rising Sun Over the Pacific." Ask for an oral or written narration.

Franklin Delano Roosevelt, U. S. president during World War II (1882–1945)

Grades 10–12: Read with your older children or assign as independent reading *America: The Last Best Hope, Volume 2,* chapter 3, "FDR and the New Deal." Ask for an oral or written narration.

Also read with your older children or assign as independent reading *American Voices,* pages 314–316, FDR's "First Inaugural Address."

World War II (1939–1945)

 # Lesson 102: World War II

Materials Needed
- *Stories of America, Vol. 2*
- *Franklin and Winston* (grades 1–3)
- *The Wright Brothers: Pioneers of American Aviation* (grades 4–6)
- *Victory in the Pacific* (grades 7–9)
- *America: The Last Best Hope, Vol. 2* (grades 10–12)

Family: Ask students what they recall about World War I and the Great Depression. Explain that smoldering hatred and discontent soon led to what some call World War I, part 2, though most people call it World War II. Read together *Stories of America, Volume 2,* chapter 26, "World War II." Ask for an oral narration.

Grades 1–3: Read with your younger children *Franklin and Winston.*

Grades 4–6: Read with your older children or assign as independent reading *The Wright Brothers: Pioneers of American Aviation,* chapter 18, "The Flying Machine." Ask for an oral or written narration.

Grades 7–9: Read with your older children or assign as independent reading *Victory in the Pacific,* chapter 2, "Wings Over Water." Ask for an oral or written narration.

Grades 10–12: Read with your older children or assign as independent reading *America: The Last Best Hope, Volume 2,* chapter 4, "America's Rendezvous with Destiny." Ask for an oral or written narration.

 # Lesson 103: Geography Book and Revelation 4

Materials Needed
- *Minn of the Mississippi* OR *WorldTrek*
- Outline map of United States; labeled U. S. map
- Bible
- *Come, Lord Jesus: Lessons from Revelation*
- *Discovering Doctrine* (grades 7–12)

Family Geography Book: Ask students what they recall from last time's reading about the Lower Mississippi and the boats that changed the River. Read together *Minn of the Mississippi,* chapters 16 and 17, and ask for an oral narration OR read together *WorldTrek,* pages 144–150, and trace the Fishers' route on a map or globe.

Family Map Drill: Give each student a copy of a blank outline map of the United States and encourage them to label the states on the map. Include the optional state abbreviations challenge if desired. Compare their labeled states with a labeled United States map and make any necessary corrections. Then have them label one or two more states on their maps, copying the spelling and locations from the labeled United States map.

Family Bible Study: Complete *Come, Lord Jesus: Lessons from Revelation*, lesson 4.

Tip: Older students should also be listening for doctrinal truths that they can add to their ongoing Discovering Doctrine *books.*

Lesson 104: The Second World War

Materials Needed
- *Stories of the Nations, Vol. 2*
- *The Little Ships* (grades 1–3)
- *Snow Treasure* (grades 4–6)
- *The Endless Steppe* (grades 7–9)
- *Hitler* (grades 10–12)

Family: Ask students what they recall about Robert Watson-Watt and his RADAR. Mention, if they do not, how his invention was in place just in time for England when it was the only country left to face the mighty Germany. Read together *Stories of the Nations, Volume 2*, chapter 20, "The Second World War." Ask for an oral narration.

Grades 1–3: Read with your younger children *The Little Ships* and ask for an oral narration.

Grades 4–6: Read with your older children or assign as independent reading *Snow Treasure*, chapters 13–15.

Grades 7–9: Read with your older children or assign as independent reading *The Endless Steppe*, chapters 8–10.

Grades 10–12: Read with your older children or assign as independent reading *Hitler*, the chapter "The Path to Power." Ask for an oral or written narration.

Lesson 105: The Underground

Materials Needed
- *Stories of the Nations, Vol. 2*
- *Always Remember Me* (grades 1–3)
- *Snow Treasure* (grades 4–6)
- *The Endless Steppe* (grades 7–9)
- *Hitler* (grades 10–12)

*Book of Centuries
Timeline*

Family: Ask students what they recall about the beginning of World War II and Hitler's Nazi Germany. Explain that, though England was the only country left to oppose Hitler in Europe, that doesn't mean that everyone else gave up. Many people in countries that he had conquered fought back in their own quiet ways. Read together *Stories of the Nations, Volume 2*, chapter 21, "The Underground." Ask for an oral narration.

Grades 1–3: Read with your younger children *Always Remember Me* and ask for an oral narration.

Tip: The grandmother in this story talks a lot about luck. You may want to discuss with your younger students the difference between luck and faith and how not all Jewish people have a relationship with God and trust Him.

Grades 4–6: Read with your older children or assign as independent reading *Snow Treasure,* chapters 16–18.

Grades 7–9: Read with your older children or assign as independent reading *The Endless Steppe,* chapters 11–13.

Grades 10–12: Read with your older children or assign as independent reading *Hitler,* the chapter "Land Without Justice." Ask for an oral or written narration.

 # Lesson 106: The Battle of the Bulge

Materials Needed
- *Stories of America, Vol. 2*
- *Rebekkah's Journey* (grades 1–3)
- *The Wright Brothers: Pioneers of American Aviation* (grades 4–6)
- *Victory in the Pacific* (grades 7–9)
- *America: The Last Best Hope, Vol. 2* (grades 10–12)
- *American Voices* (grades 10–12)

Family: Ask students what they recall about how America got involved in World War II. Explain that American soldiers fought in some important battles of that war. Read together *Stories of America, Volume 2,* chapter 27, "The Battle of the Bulge." Ask for an oral narration.

Grades 1–3: Read with your younger children *Rebekkah's Journey.*

Grades 4–6: Read with your older children or assign as independent reading *The Wright Brothers: Pioneers of American Aviation,* chapter 19, "Airplane in a Cow Pasture." Ask for an oral or written narration.

Grades 7–9: Read with your older children or assign as independent reading *Victory in the Pacific,* chapter 3, "The Canal." Ask for an oral or written narration.

Grades 10–12: Read with your older children or assign as independent reading *America: The Last Best Hope, Volume 2,* chapter 5, "Leading the Grand Alliance." Ask for an oral or written narration.

Also read with your older children or assign as independent reading *American Voices,* pages 318 and 319, FDR's "Declaration of War Speech."

Lesson 107: The Battle of Iwo Jima

Materials Needed
- *Stories of America, Vol. 2*
- *Lily's Victory Garden* (grades 1–3)
- *The Wright Brothers: Pioneers of American Aviation* (grades 4–6)
- *Victory in the Pacific* (grades 7–12)

Family: Ask students what they recall about the Battle of the Bulge. Remind students that America fought World War II on two fronts: in Europe and in the Pacific Ocean. Read together *Stories of America, Volume 2,* chapter 28, "The Battle of Iwo Jima." Ask for an oral narration. Also read the poem "The Flag Goes By," on page 179.

Tip: If students don't make the connection, remind them of the statue they saw in Our Country's Presidents *in the Franklin Delano Roosevelt section. That statue was designed after the famous photograph mentioned in this chapter of* Stories of America, Volume 2.

Grades 1–3: Read with your younger children *Lily's Victory Garden.*

Grades 4–6: Read with your older children or assign as independent reading *The Wright Brothers: Pioneers of American Aviation,* chapter 20, "Fame and Success." Ask for an oral or written narration.

Grades 7–9: Read with your older children or assign as independent reading *Victory in the Pacific,* chapter 4, "Sun, Sand, Coral, and Blood." Ask for an oral or written narration.

Grades 10–12: Read with your older children or assign as independent reading *Victory in the Pacific,* chapter 1, "Rising Sun Over the Pacific." Ask for an oral or written narration.

Tip: Make sure older children are up to date with their Book of Centuries entries.

Reminder: Start gathering the resources you will need for Term 3. See pages 103 and 104.

Reminder: If you want to do the optional hands-on project for lesson 116, start collecting the materials you will need.

Lesson 108: Geography Book and Revelation 5

Materials Needed
- *Minn of the Mississippi* OR *WorldTrek*
- Outline map of United States; labeled U. S. map
- Bible
- *Come, Lord Jesus: Lessons from Revelation*
- *Discovering Doctrine* (grades 7–12)

Family Geography Book: Ask students what they recall from last time's reading about Minn's escape and the two kinds of floods she experienced. Read together *Minn of the Mississippi*, chapters 18 and 19, and ask for an oral narration OR read together *WorldTrek*, pages 150–155, and trace the Fishers' route on a map or globe.

Family Map Drill: Give each student a copy of a blank outline map of the United States and encourage them to label the states on the map. Include the optional state abbreviations challenge if desired. Compare their labeled states with a labeled United States map and make any necessary corrections. Then have them label one or two more states on their maps, copying the spelling and locations from the labeled United States map.

Family Bible Study: Complete *Come, Lord Jesus: Lessons from Revelation*, lesson 5.

Tip: Older students should also be listening for doctrinal truths that they can add to their ongoing Discovering Doctrine *books.*

Lesson 109: World War II continued

Materials Needed
- *The Journey That Saved Curious George* (grades 1–3)
- *Snow Treasure* (grades 4–6)
- *The Endless Steppe* (grades 7–9)
- *Hitler* (grades 10–12)

Grades 1–3: Read with your younger children *The Journey That Saved Curious George*, Part I.

Grades 4–6: Read with your older children or assign as independent reading *Snow Treasure*, chapters 19–21.

Grades 7–9: Read with your older children or assign as independent reading *The Endless Steppe*, chapters 14 and 15.

Grades 10–12: Read with your older children or assign as independent

reading *Hitler*, the chapter "The March of Conquest." Ask for an oral or written narration.

Tip: *If your grade 10–12 students would like to read a powerful first-person account of life in a concentration camp, written from a Christian point of view, give them* The Hiding Place *by Corrie Ten Boom.*

 # Lesson 110: World War II continued

Materials Needed
- *The Journey That Saved Curious George* (grades 1–3)
- *Snow Treasure* (grades 4–6)
- *The Endless Steppe* (grades 7–9)
- *Hitler* (grades 10–12)

Grades 1–3: Read with your younger children *The Journey That Saved Curious George*, Part II.

Grades 4–6: Read with your older children or assign as independent reading *Snow Treasure,* chapters 22–24.

Grades 7–9: Read with your older children or assign as independent reading *The Endless Steppe,* chapters 16 and 17.

Grades 10–12: Read with your older children or assign as independent reading *Hitler*, the chapter "Barbarossa." Ask for an oral or written narration.

 # Lesson 111: V for Victory

Materials Needed
- *Stories of America, Vol. 2*
- *The Unbreakable Code* (grades 1–3)
- *Victory in the Pacific* (grades 7–12)

Family: Ask students what they recall about the Battle of Iwo Jima. Read together *Stories of America, Volume 2,* chapter 29, "V for Victory." Ask for an oral narration.

Grades 1–3: Read with your younger children *The Unbreakable Code.*

Grades 7–9: Read with your older children or assign as independent reading *Victory in the Pacific*, chapter 5, "The Silent Service." Ask for an oral or written narration.

Grades 10–12: Read with your older children or assign as independent reading *Victory in the Pacific*, chapter 2, "Wings Over Water." Ask for an oral or written narration.

Lesson 112: Harry Truman

Materials Needed
- *Our Country's Presidents*
- *Victory in the Pacific* (grades 7–12)

Family: Look together at *Our Country's Presidents,* the section on Harry S. Truman. Younger students may look at the photographs and captions; older students may read the biographical sketch if desired.

Grades 7–9: Read with your older children or assign as independent reading *Victory in the Pacific*, chapter 6, "Imperial Sunset." Ask for an oral or written narration.

Grades 10–12: Read with your older children or assign as independent reading *Victory in the Pacific*, chapter 3, "The Canal." Ask for an oral or written narration.

Tip: If appropriate, you might help your children identify any relatives or family friends who were alive during World War II. It might be interesting to ask those people what they remember about that time in American history.

Keep this idea in mind as you continue to move through the years of modern history. An interview with a relative or friend who was there as events occurred can be a valuable living resource.

Lesson 113: Geography Book and Revelation 6

Materials Needed
- *Minn of the Mississippi* OR *WorldTrek*
- Outline map of United States; labeled U. S. map
- Bible
- *Come, Lord Jesus: Lessons from Revelation*
- *Discovering Doctrine* (grades 7–12)

Family Geography Book: Ask students what they recall from last time's reading about how Minn came to the end of the River. Read together *Minn of the Mississippi*, chapter 20, and ask for an oral narration OR read together *WorldTrek*, pages 156–161, and trace the Fishers' route on a map or globe.

Family Map Drill: Give each student a copy of a blank outline map of the United States and encourage them to label the states on the map. Include the optional state abbreviations challenge if desired. Compare their labeled states with a labeled United States map and make any necessary corrections. Then have them label one or two more states on their maps, copying the spelling and locations from the labeled United States map.

Family Bible Study: Complete *Come, Lord Jesus: Lessons from Revelation*, lesson 6.

Tip: Older students should also be listening for doctrinal truths that they can add to their ongoing Discovering Doctrine books.

 # Lesson 114: The Day of Days
Materials Needed
- *Stories of the Nations, Vol. 2*
- *Snow Treasure* (grades 4–6)
- *The Endless Steppe* (grades 7–9)
- *Hitler* (grades 10–12)

Family: Ask students what they recall about World War II. Read together *Stories of the Nations, Volume 2*, chapter 22, "The Day of Days." Ask for an oral narration.

Grades 4–6: Read with your older children or assign as independent reading *Snow Treasure,* chapters 25–27.

Grades 7–9: Read with your older children or assign as independent reading *The Endless Steppe,* chapters 18 and 19.

Grades 10–12: Read with your older children or assign as independent reading *Hitler,* the chapter "Slave Empire." Ask for an oral or written narration.

 # Lesson 115: A Useful Accident
Materials Needed
- *Stories of the Nations, Vol. 2*
- *Snow Treasure* (grades 4–6)
- *The Endless Steppe* (grades 7–9)
- *Hitler* (grades 10–12)

Family: Ask students what they recall about the end of World War II. Explain that today's story is about a scientist who discovered something that saved many lives during the war. Read together *Stories of the Nations, Volume 2*, chapter 23, "A Useful Accident." Ask for an oral narration.

Grades 4–6: Read with your older children or assign as independent reading *Snow Treasure,* chapters 28–30.

Grades 7–9: Read with your older children or assign as independent reading *The Endless Steppe,* chapters 20–22.

Alexander Fleming discovers penicillium and begins work on penicillum (1928)

Grades 10–12: Read with your older children or assign as independent reading *Hitler,* the chapter "Smashing the Third Reich." Ask for an oral or written narration.

 Lesson 116: American History Project or Exam

Materials Needed
- *Victory in the Pacific* (grades 10–12)

Family: Do a hands-on project (see below), or use the questions below to begin the students' exam on American history.

Grades 1–3: Tell about a person or event from your reading that helped America learn how to do things better after that. It might be a happy or a sad story.
Grades 4–6: Tell the story of the Wright Brothers.
Grades 7–9: Describe life in America right before World War I and compare it to life between World War I and World War II.
Grades 10–12: Explain in full how or why America got involved in World War I and World War II.

Optional Hands-On Project: Select a hands-on project from the Links and Tips page: http://simplycharlottemason.com/books/modern/links-tips/

Grades 10–12: Read with your older children or assign as independent reading *Victory in the Pacific,* chapter 4, "Sun, Sand, Coral, and Blood." Ask for an oral or written narration.

Lesson 117: American History Project or Exam

Materials Needed
- *Victory in the Pacific* (grades 10–12)

Family: Finish your selected hands-on project, or use the questions below to continue the students' exam on American history.

Grades 1–3: Tell what you remember from your reading about the people involved in World War II; for example, the soldiers, those who fled their homelands, families still at home, or the heads of countries.
Grades 4–6: Tell a story from World War I or World War II.
Grades 7–9: "A date which will live in infamy": Describe in full who said this phrase, of what that person was speaking, and the events that followed.
Grades 10–12: What was the cause of the Great Depression in America and

how did World War II help put an end to it?

Grades 10–12: Read with your older children or assign as independent reading *Victory in the Pacific*, chapters 5 and 6, "The Silent Service" and "Imperial Sunset." Ask for an oral or written narration.

Lesson 118: Geography and Bible Exams

Family Geography Exam: Use the questions below according to the book you have been reading.

Minn of the Mississippi: Trace on a map where the Mississippi River flows in America and tell about what you would see as you travel down it.
WorldTrek: Select two of the countries the Fishers have visited in the book and tell all you remember about each: Germany, France, Italy, Greece, Turkey, Egypt.

Map Drill: Give each student a copy of a blank outline map of the United States and ask them to label as many of the states as they can. Include the optional abbreviations challenge if desired.

Bible Exam: Tell something you have learned from your study of Revelation that you did not know before.

Lesson 119: World History Exam

Family: Use the questions below to begin the students' exam on Modern world history.

Grades 1–3: Tell the story of a discovery by an explorer or a scientist about which you read this term.
Grades 4–6: Tell in full what life was like for soldiers during World War I.
Grades 7–9: Describe World War I: its causes, its participants, its scope, and its end.
Grades 10–12: Explain how World War II could be considered a continuation of World War I.

Lesson 120: World History Exam

Family: Use the questions below to continue the students' exam on Modern world history.

Grades 1–3: Tell the story of someone about whom you read this term who

*Book of Centuries
Timeline*

had to flee their country because of war.

Grades 4–6: Describe how groups of civilians quietly fought against Hitler and Nazi Germany in World War II.

Grades 7–9: Describe World War II: its causes, its participants, its scope, and its end.

Grades 10–12: Discuss the difference between a dictatorship and a totalitarian government. Which description best fits Hitler's government? Support your answer with examples from your reading.

Term 3
(12 weeks; 5 lessons/week)

American History Resources
- *Stories of America, Volume 2*, by Charles Morris, et al.
- Copy of "I Have a Dream" speech
- *Billy Graham: God's Ambassador* by Russ Busby
OR *Billy Graham: Just Get Up Out of Your Seat* by Catherine Mackenzie
- *Our Country's Presidents* by Ann Bausum (reference book)

Grades 1–3
- *I Have a Dream: The Story of Martin Luther King* by Margaret Davidson
- *Moonshot: The Flight of Apollo 11* by Brian Floca

Grades 4–6
- *I Have a Dream: The Story of Martin Luther King* by Margaret Davidson
- *Team Moon: How 400,000 People Landed Apollo 11 on the Moon* by Catherine Thimmesh
- *Our Country's Presidents* by Ann Bausum (reference book)

Grades 7–9
- *Roll of Thunder, Hear My Cry* by Mildred D. Taylor
- *Ronald Reagan: Destiny at His Side* by Janet and Geoff Benge
- Book of Centuries (one for each student)

Grades 10–12
- *America: The Last Best Hope, Volume 2: From a World at War to the Triumph of Freedom* by William Bennett
- *Freedom Walkers* by Russell Freedman
- *America: The Last Best Hope, Volume 3: From the Collapse of Communism to the Rise of Radical Islam* by William Bennett
- *American Voices* edited by Ray Notgrass
- Book of Centuries (one for each student)

Optional Resources
- Dover coloring books
- Various resources for optional hands-on projects

World History, Bible, Geography Resources
- *Stories of the Nations, Volume 2*, by Lorene Lambert
- *Gandhi: The Young Protester Who Founded a Nation* by Philip Wilkinson
- *Mandela: The Rebel Who Led His Nation to Freedom* by Ann Kramer
- *Come, Lord Jesus: Lessons from Revelation* by Sonya Shafer
- Bible
- *Paddle to the Sea* by Holling C. Holling
OR *WorldTrek* by Russell and Carla Fisher
- *Uncle Josh's Outline Map book or CD* by George and Hannah Wiggers (United States)
- Labeled United States map

Grades 1–3
(No additional reading this term)

Grades 4–6
- *Brother Andrew: God's Secret Agent* by Janet and Geoff Benge

Grades 7–9
- *Animal Farm* by George Orwell
- *Rescue and Redeem: Volume 5: Chronicles of the Modern Church* by Mindy and Brandon Withrow
- *Swifter, Higher, Stronger: A Photographic History of the Summer Olympics* by Sue Macy
- *Discovering Doctrine* by Sonya Shafer (one for each student)
- Book of Centuries (one for each student)

Grades 10–12
- *Stalin: Russia's Man of Steel* by Albert Marrin
- *Rescue and Redeem: Volume 5: Chronicles of the Modern Church* by Mindy and Brandon Withrow
- *How Should We Then Live?* by Francis A Schaeffer
OR *7 Men Who Rule the World from the Grave* by Dave Breese
- *Discovering Doctrine* by Sonya Shafer (one for each student)
- Book of Centuries (one for each student)

Optional Resources
- Dover coloring books

	Family	Grades 1–3	4–6	7–9	10–12
Week 1, Lessons 121–125					
American History	Stories of America, Vol. 2, ch. 30	I Have a Dream, pp. 5–36	I Have a Dream, pp. 5–36	Roll of Thunder, ch. 1, 2	America, Vol. 2, ch. 6, 7; American Voices, pp. 320–328
Geography	Paddle to the Sea, ch. 1–3, OR WorldTrek, pp. 161–167; Map Drill: United States				
Bible	Revelation study, lesson 7				Discovering Doctrine summary
World History	Stories of the Nations, Vol. 2, ch. 24, 25		Brother Andrew, ch. 1, 2	Rescue and Redeem, pp. 149–192	Rescue and Redeem, pp. 149–192
Week 2, Lessons 126–130					
American History	Our Country's Presidents	I Have a Dream, pp. 38–75	I Have a Dream, pp. 38–75	Roll of Thunder, ch. 3, 4	America, Vol. 2, ch. 8, 9A; American Voices, pp. 329–339
Geography	Paddle to the Sea, ch. 4, 5, OR WorldTrek, pp. 167–174; Map Drill: United States				
Bible	Revelation study, lesson 8				Discovering Doctrine summary
World History	Gandhi, pp. 6–21		Brother Andrew, ch. 3, 4	Animal Farm, ch. 1, 2	Stalin, Prologue–ch. 2
Week 3, Lessons 131–135					
American History	Stories of America, Vol. 2, ch. 31 and poem; I Have a Dream speech	I Have a Dream, pp. 76–103	I Have a Dream, pp. 76–103	Roll of Thunder, ch. 5, 6	America, Vol. 2, ch. 9B; American Voices, pp. 340–350; Freedom Walkers, Intro–ch. 4
Geography	Paddle to the Sea, ch. 6–8, OR WorldTrek, pp. 175–178; Map Drill: United States				
Bible	Revelation study, lesson 9				Discovering Doctrine summary
World History	Gandhi, pp. 22–41		Brother Andrew, ch. 5, 6	Animal Farm, ch. 3, 4	Stalin, ch. 3
Week 4, Lessons 136–140					
American History	Our Country's Presidents; Stories of America, Vol. 2, ch. 32	I Have a Dream, pp. 104–127; Moonshot	I Have a Dream, pp. 104–127; Team Moon, pp. 4–17	Roll of Thunder, ch. 7, 8	Freedom Walkers, ch. 5–8; American Voices, p. 354; America, Vol. 2, ch. 10A
Geography	Paddle to the Sea, ch. 9, 10, OR WorldTrek, pp. 178–185; Map Drill: United States				
Bible	Revelation study, lesson 10				Discovering Doctrine summary
World History	Gandhi, pp. 42–59		Brother Andrew, ch. 7, 8	Animal Farm, ch. 5, 6	Stalin, ch. 4, 5A

Week 5, Lessons 141–145					
American History	Billy Graham		Team Moon, pp. 18–41	Roll of Thunder, ch. 9, 10	America, Vol. 2, ch. 10B, 11; American Voices, pp. 356–366
Geography	Paddle to the Sea, ch. 11–13, OR WorldTrek, pp. 185–188; Map Drill: United States				
Bible	Revelation study, lesson 11				Discovering Doctrine summary
World History	Stories of the Nations, Vol. 2, ch. 26, 27		Brother Andrew, ch. 9, 10	Animal Farm, ch. 7, 8	Stalin, ch. 5B, 6A
Week 6, Lessons 146–150					
American History	Billy Graham		Team Moon, pp. 42–69	Roll of Thunder, ch. 11, 12; Ronald Reagan, ch. 1, 2	America, Vol. 2, ch. 12; American Voices, pp. 367–375
Geography	Paddle to the Sea, ch. 14, 15, OR WorldTrek, pp. 189–195; Map Drill: United States				
Bible	Revelation study, lesson 12				Discovering Doctrine summary
World History	Stories of the Nations, Vol. 2, ch. 28, 29		Brother Andrew, ch. 11, 12	Animal Farm, ch. 9, 10	Stalin, ch. 6B, 7
Week 7, Lessons 151–155					
American History	Stories of America, Vol. 2, ch. 33; Our Country's Presidents; Billy Graham		Our Country's Presidents, project	Ronald Reagan, ch. 3–6	America, Vol. 3, ch. 1
Geography	Paddle to the Sea, ch. 16–18, OR WorldTrek, pp. 195–203; Map Drill: United States				
Bible	Revelation study, lesson 13				Discovering Doctrine summary
World History	Stories of the Nations, Vol. 2, ch. 30; Mandela, pp. 6–15		Brother Andrew, ch. 13, 14	Rescue and Redeem, pp. 193–216	Rescue and Redeem, pp. 193–216
Week 8, Lessons 156–160					
American History	Stories of America, Vol. 2, ch. 34; Our Country's Presidents; Billy Graham		Our Country's Presidents, project	Ronald Reagan, ch. 7–10	America, Vol. 3, ch. 2
Geography	Paddle to the Sea, ch. 19, 20, OR WorldTrek, pp. 203–211; Map Drill: United States				
Bible	Revelation study, lesson 14				Discovering Doctrine summary
World History	Mandela, pp. 16–35		Brother Andrew, ch. 15, 16	Rescue and Redeem, pp. 217–244	Rescue and Redeem, pp. 217–244

Week 9, Lessons 161–165				
American History	Stories of America, Vol. 2, ch. 35; Billy Graham		Our Country's Presidents, project	Ronald Reagan, ch. 11–14	America, Vol. 3, ch. 3, 4A; American Voices, pp. 386–392
Geography	Paddle to the Sea, ch. 21–23, OR WorldTrek, pp. 212–217; Map Drill: United States				
Bible	Revelation study, lesson 15				Discovering Doctrine summary
World History	Mandela, pp. 36–51		Brother Andrew, ch. 17, 18	Swifter, Higher, Stronger, ch. 1, 2	How Should We Then Live, ch. 8, 9 OR 7 Men Who Rule, ch. 7, 8
Week 10, Lessons 166–170				
American History	Stories of America, Vol. 2, ch. 36; Billy Graham		Our Country's Presidents, project	Ronald Reagan, ch. 15–18	America, Vol. 3, ch. 4B, 5
Geography	Paddle to the Sea, ch. 24, 25, OR WorldTrek, pp. 217–223; Map Drill: United States				
Bible	Revelation study, lesson 16				Discovering Doctrine summary
World History	Mandela, pp. 52–59; Stories of the Nations, Vol. 2, ch. 31			Swifter, Higher, Stronger, ch. 3, 4	How Should We Then Live, ch. 10, 11 OR 7 Men Who Rule, ch. 9, 10
Week 11, Lessons 171–175				
American History	Billy Graham; poem		Our Country's Presidents, project	Ronald Reagan, ch. 19, 20	America, Vol. 3, ch. 6
Geography	Paddle to the Sea, ch. 26, 27, OR WorldTrek, pp. 224–228; Map Drill: United States				
Bible	Revelation study, lesson 17				Discovering Doctrine summary
World History	Stories of the Nations, Vol. 2, ch. 32			Swifter, Higher, Stronger, ch. 5	How Should We Then Live, ch. 12, 13 OR 7 Men Who Rule, ch. 11, 12
Week 12, Lessons 176–180				
American History	Exam or Project				America, Vol. 3, Epilogue
Geography	Exam				
Bible	Exam				
World History	Exam				

Lesson 121: A Long Cold War

Materials Needed

- *Stories of America, Vol. 2*
- *I Have a Dream* (grades 1–6)
- *Roll of Thunder, Hear My Cry* (grades 7–9)
- *America: The Last Best Hope, Vol. 2* (grades 10–12)

Family: Ask students what they recall about World War II. Read together *Stories of America, Volume 2*, chapter 30, "A Long Cold War," and ask for an oral narration.

Cold War between Soviet Union and U. S. (approx. 1945–1991)

Grades 1–6: Read with your children or assign to older children as independent reading *I Have a Dream,* pages 5–17, "You Are as Good as Anyone" and "I'm Going to Get Me Some Big Words." Ask for an oral or written narration.

Grades 7–9: Read with your older children or assign as independent reading *Roll of Thunder, Hear My Cry,* chapter 1. Ask for an oral or written narration if desired.

Grades 10–12: Read with your older children or assign as independent reading *America: The Last Best Hope, Volume 2,* chapter 6, "America Victorious." Ask for an oral or written narration.

 # Lesson 122: Various Readings

Materials Needed

- *I Have a Dream* (grades 1–6)
- *Roll of Thunder, Hear My Cry* (grades 7–9)
- *America: The Last Best Hope, Vol. 2* (grades 10–12)
- *American Voices* (grades 10–12)

Grades 1–6: Read with your children or assign to older children as independent reading *I Have a Dream,* pages 18–36, "A Dream Begins to Grow" and "Some Big Ideas." Ask for an oral or written narration.

Grades 7–9: Read with your older children or assign as independent reading *Roll of Thunder, Hear My Cry,* chapter 2. Ask for an oral or written narration if desired.

Grades 10–12: Read with your older children or assign as independent reading *America: The Last Best Hope, Volume 2,* chapter 7, "Truman Defends the Free World." Ask for an oral or written narration.

Also read together or assign as independent reading *American Voices,* pages 320–328, "Old Soldiers Never Die" and "Harry S. Truman's Farewell Address." If desired, you may be able to find an audio recording of these speeches on the Internet.

Reminder: Find a copy of Martin Luther King's "I Have a Dream" speech either in printed or audio format for lesson 132. You should be able to find either on the Internet. If you have American Voices *for grades 10–12, you will find a printed copy on page 351. Also get the book* Freedom Walkers *for grades 10–12 for lesson 132.*

Lesson 123: Geography Book and Revelation 7

Materials Needed

- *Paddle to the Sea* OR *WorldTrek*
- Outline map of United States; labeled U. S. map
- Bible
- *Come, Lord Jesus: Lessons from Revelation*
- *Discovering Doctrine* (grades 7–12)

Family Geography Book: Read together *Paddle to the Sea*, chapters 1–3, and ask for an oral narration OR read together *WorldTrek*, pages 161–167, and trace the Fishers' route on a map or globe.

Tip: The Indian boy in Paddle to the Sea, *chapter 2, talks about the Sun Spirit, rather than just the sun. Feel free to change the wording or read it as is and discuss the Indian boy's beliefs.*

Family Map Drill: Give each student a copy of a blank outline map of the United States and encourage them to label the states on the map. Include the optional state abbreviations challenge if desired. Compare their labeled states with a labeled United States map and make any necessary corrections. Then have them label one or two more states on their maps, copying the spelling and locations from the labeled United States map.

Family Bible Study: Complete *Come, Lord Jesus: Lessons from Revelation*, lesson 7.

Grades 10–12: Older students who have searched Genesis through Jude for doctrinal truths and recorded them in their *Discovering Doctrine* books may begin to summarize their findings for each of the ten doctrines. Ask them to summarize their Bibliology findings this week in written form. They should also record their findings from the Revelation study under Eschatology (which will be summarized last, after completing the Revelation study).

Tip: Those older students who are not summarizing Discovering Doctrine *findings this term should still record doctrinal truths from* Revelation.

Lesson 124: The Creation of Israel

Materials Needed
- *Stories of the Nations, Vol. 2*
- *Brother Andrew* (grades 4–6)
- *Rescue and Redeem* (grades 7–12)

Family: Help students locate the nation of Israel on a world map or globe. Read together *Stories of the Nations, Volume 2,* chapter 24, "The Creation of Israel." Ask for an oral narration.

Grades 4–6: Read with your older children or assign as independent reading *Brother Andrew,* chapter 1, "At the Border." Ask for an oral or written narration.

Tip: Depending on the maturity level of your student, you may want to read Brother Andrew *to or with your child so you can discuss the events. In particular, there is a section in chapter 6 that describes when Andrew was serving as a soldier in Indonesia and saw a mother and baby killed. That image disturbed him for a time, and more sensitive students may need to have that part skipped or at least mentioned ahead of time.*

Jews return to Palestine and nation of Israel is recognized (1948)

Grades 7–12: Read with your older children or assign as independent reading *Rescue and Redeem,* pages 149–170, "The Bible in New Words" and "Marianna Slocum." Ask for an oral or written narration.

Reminder: Make sure you have the books Gandhi: The Young Protester Who Founded a Nation *for Family,* Animal Farm *for grades 7–9, and* Stalin *for grades 10–12 for lesson 129.*

 # Lesson 125: The Dead Sea Scrolls

Materials Needed
- *Stories of the Nations, Vol. 2*
- *Brother Andrew* (grades 4–6)
- *Rescue and Redeem* (grades 7–12)

Family: Ask students what they recall about the creation of the nation of Israel. Read together *Stories of the Nations, Volume 2,* chapter 25, "The Dead Sea Scrolls." Ask for an oral narration.

Grades 4–6: Read with your older children or assign as independent reading *Brother Andrew,* chapter 2, "Pretend Spy." Ask for an oral or written narration.

Grades 7–12: Read with your older children or assign as independent

Shepherd boy discovers the Dead Sea Scrolls (1947)

reading *Rescue and Redeem,* pages 171–192, "Dietrich Bonhoeffer." Ask for an oral or written narration.

 Lesson 126: Dwight Eisenhower

Materials Needed
- *Our Country's Presidents*
- *I Have a Dream* (grades 1–6)
- *Roll of Thunder, Hear My Cry* (grades 7–9)
- *America: The Last Best Hope, Vol. 2* (grades 10–12)
- *American Voices* (grades 10–12)

Family: Look at *Our Country's Presidents*, the section on Dwight D. Eisenhower. Younger students can learn from the photograph captions; older students may read the biographical sketch.

Grades 1–6: Read with your children or assign to older children as independent reading *I Have a Dream,* pages 38–60, "The Man and the Movement Meet" and "The Walking City." Ask for an oral or written narration.

Grades 7–9: Read with your older children or assign as independent reading *Roll of Thunder, Hear My Cry,* chapter 3. Ask for an oral or written narration if desired.

Grades 10–12: Read with your older children or assign as independent reading *America: The Last Best Hope, Volume 2,* chapter 8, "Eisenhower and Happy Days." Ask for an oral or written narration.

Also read together or assign as independent reading *American Voices,* pages 329–336, "Brown v. Board of Education" and "Dwight D. Eisenhower's Farewell Address." If desired, you may be able to find an audio recording of Eisenhower's speech on the Internet.

 Lesson 127: John F. Kennedy

Materials Needed
- *Our Country's Presidents*
- *I Have a Dream* (grades 1–6)
- *Roll of Thunder, Hear My Cry* (grades 7–9)
- *America: The Last Best Hope, Vol. 2* (grades 10–12)
- *American Voices* (grades 10–12)

Family: Look at *Our Country's Presidents*, the section on John F. Kennedy. Younger students can learn from the photograph captions; older students may read the biographical sketch.

Grades 1–6: Read with your children or assign to older children as independent reading *I Have a Dream*, pages 61–75, "The Miracle of Montgomery" and "The Movement Grows." Ask for an oral or written narration.

Grades 7–9: Read with your older children or assign as independent reading *Roll of Thunder, Hear My Cry*, chapter 4. Ask for an oral or written narration if desired.

Grades 10–12: Read with your older children or assign as independent reading *America: The Last Best Hope, Volume 2,* the first half of chapter 9, "Passing the Torch," approximately pages 335–361. Ask for an oral or written narration.

Also read together or assign as independent reading *American Voices*, pages 337–339, "John F. Kennedy's Inaugural Address." If desired, you may be able to find an audio recording of this speech on the Internet.

Tip: Make sure older children are up to date with their Book of Centuries entries.

Reminder: Get the books Moonshot *for grades 1–3 and* Team Moon *for grades 4–6 for lesson 137. You will also need either* Billy Graham: God's Ambassador *OR* Billy Graham: Just Get Up Out of Your Seat *for Family for lesson 141.*

Lesson 128: Geography Book and Revelation 8

Materials Needed
- *Paddle to the Sea* OR *WorldTrek*
- Outline map of United States; labeled U. S. map
- Bible
- *Come, Lord Jesus: Lessons from Revelation*
- *Discovering Doctrine* (grades 7–12)

Family Geography Book: Ask students what they recall from last time's reading about Paddle-to-the-Sea's creation and launch. Read together *Paddle to the Sea*, chapters 4 and 5, and ask for an oral narration OR read together *WorldTrek*, pages 167–174, and trace the Fishers' route on a map or globe.

Tip: Be sure to refer often to the map in the back of Paddle to the Sea *to trace his route.*

Family Map Drill: Give each student a copy of a blank outline map of the United States and encourage them to label the states on the map. Include the optional state abbreviations challenge if desired. Compare their

Book of Centuries Timeline

labeled states with a labeled United States map and make any necessary corrections. Then have them label one or two more states on their maps, copying the spelling and locations from the labeled United States map.

Family Bible Study: Complete *Come, Lord Jesus: Lessons from Revelation*, lesson 8.

Grades 10–12: Older students who are completing *Discovering Doctrine* this year should summarize their Theology Proper findings this week in written form. They should also record their findings from the Revelation study under Eschatology.

Tip: Those older students who are not summarizing Discovering Doctrine *findings this term should still record doctrinal truths from* Revelation.

 # Lesson 129: Gandhi, part 1

Materials Needed
- *Gandhi: The Young Protester Who Founded a Nation*
- *Brother Andrew* (grades 4–6)
- *Animal Farm* (grades 7–9)
- *Stalin: Russia's Man of Steel* (grades 10–12)

Family: Help students locate India on a world map or globe. Ask students what they know about India. Explain that they will be reading about a man who led that country to independence. Read together *Gandhi*, pages 6–15, from "A Prime Minister's Son" to "The Raj." Ask for an oral narration.

Grades 4–6: Read with your older children or assign as independent reading *Brother Andrew*, chapter 3, "Something Sinister Was Creeping over Europe." Ask for an oral or written narration.

Grades 7–9: Read with your older children or assign as independent reading *Animal Farm*, chapter 1. Ask for an oral or written narration.

Tip: Explain to your grades 7–9 students that Animal Farm *was originally called a fairy story, or fairy tale. It was written to warn of the dangers of socialism and to expose how Stalin had taken advantage of the Russian Revolution to promote his brutal agenda. Encourage students to consider what they are reading and to look for modern day comparisons; in other words, to learn the lessons of* Animal Farm.

Grades 10–12: Read with your older children or assign as independent reading *Stalin*, the Prologue and "The Rebel." Ask for an oral or written narration.

Gandhi protests for India's freedom from British rule (1869–1948)

Lesson 130: Gandhi, part 2

Materials Needed
- *Gandhi: The Young Protester Who Founded a Nation*
- *Brother Andrew* (grades 4–6)
- *Animal Farm* (grades 7–9)
- *Stalin* (grades 10–12)

Family: Ask students what they recall from last time's reading about Gandhi's childhood and India's history. Read together *Gandhi*, pages 16–21, from "On the Move" to "Religion or Rebellion?" Ask for an oral narration.

Tip: The first sentence on page 20, at the beginning of the "Religion or Rebellion?" section, presents an assumption about teenagers that you might want to discuss with your children.

Grades 4–6: Read with your older children or assign as independent reading *Brother Andrew,* chapter 4, "Resistance." Ask for an oral or written narration.

Grades 7–9: Read with your older children or assign as independent reading *Animal Farm,* chapter 2. Ask for an oral or written narration.

Grades 10–12: Read with your older children or assign as independent reading *Stalin,* the chapter "Stepping Stones to Power." Ask for an oral or written narration.

 # Lesson 131: Civil Rights

Materials Needed
- *Stories of America, Vol. 2*
- *I Have a Dream* (grades 1–6)
- *Roll of Thunder, Hear My Cry* (grades 7–9)
- *America: The Last Best Hope, Vol. 2* (grades 10–12)
- *American Voices* (grades 10–12)

Family: Read together *Stories of America, Volume 2*, chapter 31, "For Civil Rights." Ask for an oral narration. Encourage students to include ideas from their independent readings as well. Also read together the poem "Sympathy" from *Stories of America, Volume 2*, page 195. Discuss how this poem, written by a black man, illustrates the heart of the Civil Rights movement.

Grades 1–6: Read with your children or assign to older children as independent reading *I Have a Dream,* pages 76–90, "The Children's Crusade." Ask for an oral or written narration.

Grades 7–9: Read with your older children or assign as independent

Civil Rights movement in U. S. led by Martin Luther King, Jr. (1955–1968)

reading *Roll of Thunder, Hear My Cry,* chapter 5. Ask for an oral or written narration if desired.

Grades 10–12: Read with your older children or assign as independent reading *America: The Last Best Hope, Volume 2,* the last half of chapter 9, "Passing the Torch," approximately pages 361–397. Ask for an oral or written narration.

Also read together or assign as independent reading *American Voices,* pages 340–350, "Letter From a Birmingham Jail."

 # Lesson 132: I Have a Dream

Materials Needed
- Copy of "I Have a Dream" speech
- *I Have a Dream* (grades 1–6)
- *Roll of Thunder, Hear My Cry* (grades 7–9)
- *Freedom Walkers* (grades 10–12)

Family: Ask students what they recall about the Civil Rights movement. Read or listen together to Martin Luther King's "I Have a Dream" speech. You should be able to find a copy and an audio recording on the Internet. If you have the book *American Voices* for grades 10–12, you will find the speech on pages 351–353.

Grades 1–6: Read with your children or assign to older children as independent reading *I Have a Dream,* pages 91–103, "I Have a Dream Today" and "The Greatest Award of All." Ask for an oral or written narration.

Grades 7–9: Read with your older children or assign as independent reading *Roll of Thunder, Hear My Cry,* chapter 6. Ask for an oral or written narration if desired.

Grades 10–12: Read with your older children or assign as independent reading *Freedom Walkers,* Introduction and chapters 1–4. Ask for an oral or written narration.

 # Lesson 133: Geography Book and Revelation 9

Materials Needed
- *Paddle to the Sea* OR *WorldTrek*
- Outline map of United States; labeled U. S. map
- Bible
- *Come, Lord Jesus: Lessons from Revelation*
- *Discovering Doctrine* (grades 7–12)

Family Geography Book: Ask students what they recall from last time's reading about Paddle-to-the-Sea's journey from brook to river. Read together *Paddle to the Sea*, chapters 6–8, and ask for an oral narration OR read together *WorldTrek*, pages 175–178, and trace the Fishers' route on a map or globe.

Family Map Drill: Give each student a copy of a blank outline map of the United States and encourage them to label the states on the map. Include the optional state abbreviations challenge if desired. Compare their labeled states with a labeled United States map and make any necessary corrections. Then have them label one or two more states on their maps, copying the spelling and locations from the labeled United States map.

Family Bible Study: Complete *Come, Lord Jesus: Lessons from Revelation*, lesson 9.

Grades 10–12: Older students who are completing *Discovering Doctrine* this year should summarize their Christology findings this week in written form. They should also record their findings from the Revelation study under Eschatology.

Tip: Those older students who are not summarizing Discovering Doctrine *findings this term should still record doctrinal truths from* Revelation.

 Lesson 134: Gandhi, part 3

Materials Needed
- *Gandhi: The Young Protester Who Founded a Nation*
- *Brother Andrew* (grades 4–6)
- *Animal Farm* (grades 7–9)
- *Stalin* (grades 10–12)

Family: Ask students what they recall from last time's reading about Gandhi's teen years. Read together *Gandhi*, pages 22–31, from "Studying Law" to "Traveling to South Africa." Ask for an oral narration.

Grades 4–6: Read with your older children or assign as independent reading *Brother Andrew,* chapter 5, "Sure That He Had Found His Future." Ask for an oral or written narration.

Grades 7–9: Read with your older children or assign as independent reading *Animal Farm*, chapter 3. Ask for an oral or written narration.

Grades 10–12: Read with your older children or assign as independent reading *Stalin*, the first half of the chapter "Workers' Paradise," approximately pages 75–95. Ask for an oral or written narration.

Lesson 135: Gandhi, part 4

Materials Needed
- *Gandhi: The Young Protester Who Founded a Nation*
- *Brother Andrew* (grades 4–6)
- *Animal Farm* (grades 7–9)
- *Stalin* (grades 10–12)

Family: Ask students what they recall from last time's reading about Gandhi's studies and travels. Read together *Gandhi*, pages 32–41, from "Peaceful Protest" to "Cloth and Spinning." Ask for an oral narration.

Grades 4–6: Read with your older children or assign as independent reading *Brother Andrew*, chapter 6, "A Searing Image." Ask for an oral or written narration.

Grades 7–9: Read with your older children or assign as independent reading *Animal Farm*, chapter 4. Ask for an oral or written narration.

Grades 10–12: Read with your older children or assign as independent reading *Stalin*, the last half of the chapter "Workers' Paradise," approximately pages 95–115. Ask for an oral or written narration.

 # Lesson 136: Lyndon B. Johnson

Materials Needed
- *Our Country's Presidents*
- *I Have a Dream* (grades 1–6)
- *Roll of Thunder, Hear My Cry* (grades 7–9)
- *Freedom Walkers* (grades 10–12)
- *American Voices* (grades 10–12)

Family: Look at *Our Country's Presidents*, the section on Lyndon B. Johnson. Younger students can learn from the photograph captions; older students may read the biographical sketch.

Grades 1–6: Read with your children or assign to older children as independent reading *I Have a Dream*, pages 104–127, the rest of the book. Ask for an oral or written narration.

Grades 7–9: Read with your older children or assign as independent reading *Roll of Thunder, Hear My Cry*, chapter 7. Ask for an oral or written narration if desired.

Grades 10–12: Read with your older children or assign as independent reading *Freedom Walkers*, chapters 5–8. Ask for an oral or written narration.
    Also read together or assign as independent reading *American Voices*, page 354, "Our God, He Is Alive."

Lesson 137: The Land of What Can Be

Materials Needed
- *Stories of America, Vol. 2*
- *Our Country's Presidents*
- *Moonshot* (grades 1–3)
- *Team Moon* (grades 4–6)
- *Roll of Thunder, Hear My Cry* (grades 7–9)
- *America: The Last Best Hope, Vol. 2* (grades 10–12)

Family: Read together *Stories of America, Volume 2*, chapter 32, "The Land of What Can Be." Ask for an oral narration. If desired, look at *Our Country's Presidents*, the section on Richard Nixon. You will find a photograph that shows what people saw on television when Nixon talked to Armstrong on the moon. Older students may read the biographical sketch.

NASA lands men on the moon, Neil Armstrong and Buzz Aldrin (1969)

> *Tip: Don't forget to include in your studies friends or family members who can give a first-hand account of watching this event as it happened.*

Grades 1–3: Read with your children or assign to older children as independent reading *Moonshot*.

Grades 4–6: Read with your older children or assign as independent reading *Team Moon,* pages 4–17. Ask for an oral or written narration if desired.

Grades 7–9: Read with your older children or assign as independent reading *Roll of Thunder, Hear My Cry,* chapter 8. Ask for an oral or written narration if desired.

Grades 10–12: Read with your older children or assign as independent reading *America: The Last Best Hope, Volume 2,* the first half of chapter 10, "Nixon's the One," approximately pages 398–422. Ask for an oral or written narration.

> *Tip: Make sure older children are up to date with their Book of Centuries entries.*

> *Reminder: Get the book* Ronald Reagan: Destiny at His Side *for grades 7–9 for lesson 147. You will also need* America The Last Best Hope, Volume 3, *for grades 10–12 for lesson 151.*

Lesson 138: Geography Book and Revelation 10

Materials Needed
- *Paddle to the Sea* OR *WorldTrek*

*Book of Centuries
Timeline*

• Outline map of United States; labeled U. S. map
• Bible
• *Come, Lord Jesus: Lessons from Revelation*
• *Discovering Doctrine* (grades 7–12)

Family Geography Book: Ask students what they recall from last time's reading about Paddle-to-the-Sea at the sawmill and Lake Superior. Read together *Paddle to the Sea*, chapters 9 and 10, and ask for an oral narration OR read together *WorldTrek*, pages 178–185, and trace the Fishers' route on a map or globe.

Family Map Drill: Give each student a copy of a blank outline map of the United States and encourage them to label the states on the map. Include the optional state abbreviations challenge if desired. Compare their labeled states with a labeled United States map and make any necessary corrections. Then have them label one or two more states on their maps, copying the spelling and locations from the labeled United States map.

Family Bible Study: Complete *Come, Lord Jesus: Lessons from Revelation*, lesson 10.

Grades 10–12: Older students who are completing *Discovering Doctrine* this year should summarize their Pneumatology findings this week in written form. They should also record their findings from the Revelation study under Eschatology.

Tip: Those older students who are not summarizing Discovering Doctrine *findings this term should still record doctrinal truths from Revelation.*

 Lesson 139: Gandhi, part 5

Materials Needed
• *Gandhi: The Young Protester Who Founded a Nation*
• *Brother Andrew* (grades 4–6)
• *Animal Farm* (grades 7–9)
• *Stalin* (grades 10–12)

Family: Ask students what they recall from last time's reading about Gandhi's return to India. Read together *Gandhi*, pages 42–51, from "From Protest to Tragedy" to "The Salt March." Ask for an oral narration.

Grades 4–6: Read with your older children or assign as independent reading *Brother Andrew*, chapter 7, "Home at Last." Ask for an oral or written narration.

Grades 7–9: Read with your older children or assign as independent reading *Animal Farm*, chapter 5. Ask for an oral or written narration.

Grades 10–12: Read with your older children or assign as independent reading *Stalin,* the chapter "Stalin's Terror." Ask for an oral or written narration.

 # Lesson 140: Gandhi, part 6

Materials Needed
  • *Gandhi: The Young Protester Who Founded a Nation*
  • *Brother Andrew* (grades 4–6)
  • *Animal Farm* (grades 7–9)
  • *Stalin* (grades 10–12)

Family: Ask students what they recall from last time's reading about Gandhi's protests. Read together *Gandhi,* pages 52–59, from "Quit India!" to "Gandhi's Achievements." Ask for an oral narration.

Grades 4–6: Read with your older children or assign as independent reading *Brother Andrew,* chapter 8, "Letting Go of Himself." Ask for an oral or written narration.

Grades 7–9: Read with your older children or assign as independent reading *Animal Farm,* chapter 6. Ask for an oral or written narration.

Grades 10–12: Read with your older children or assign as independent reading *Stalin,* the first half of the chapter "The Pact of Blood," approximately pages 146–160. Ask for an oral or written narration.

 # Lesson 141: Billy Graham, part 1

Materials Needed
  • *Billy Graham: God's Ambassador* OR *Just Get Up Out of Your Seat*
  • *Team Moon* (grades 4–6)
  • *Roll of Thunder, Hear My Cry* (grades 7–9)
  • *America: The Last Best Hope, Vol. 2* (grades 10–12)
  • *American Voices* (grades 10–12)

Family: For a quick review, mention each of the following names or events, one at a time, and ask students what they remember about them: Franklin D. Roosevelt, World War II, the Cold War, Martin Luther King, Jr., Civil Rights, Neil Armstrong, NASA.
  Explain that one man who lived through these events about which you have been reading is Billy Graham. Read together *Billy Graham: God's Ambassador,* the first half of chapter 1, "Shaping a Life," approximately pages 19–27, OR *Just Get Up Out of Your Seat*, pages 11–20, "Fancy Ties and Tarzan Games" and "It's all Hogwash." Ask for an oral narration if desired.

Tip: Both books on Billy Graham are good. Billy Graham: God's Ambassador *reads like a scrapbook with numerous photographs and souvenirs from across the years that make Rev. Graham's life come alive.* Just Get Up Out of Your Seat *reads more like a story.*

Grades 4–6: Read with your older children or assign as independent reading *Team Moon,* pages 18–29. Ask for an oral or written narration if desired.

Grades 7–9: Read with your older children or assign as independent reading *Roll of Thunder, Hear My Cry,* chapter 9. Ask for an oral or written narration if desired.

Grades 10–12: Read with your older children or assign as independent reading *America: The Last Best Hope, Volume 2,* the last half of chapter 10, "Nixon's the One," approximately pages 422–443. Ask for an oral or written narration.

Also read together or assign as independent reading *American Voices,* pages 356–362, "Roe v. Wade." Ask for an oral or written narration.

Lesson 142: Billy Graham, part 2

Materials Needed
- *Billy Graham: God's Ambassador* OR *Just Get Up Out of Your Seat*
- *Team Moon* (grades 4–6)
- *Roll of Thunder, Hear My Cry* (grades 7–9)
- *America: The Last Best Hope, Vol. 2* (grades 10–12)
- *American Voices* (grades 10–12)

Family: Ask students what they recall about Billy Graham's life so far. Read together *Billy Graham: God's Ambassador,* the last half of chapter 1, "Shaping a Life," approximately pages 28–37, OR *Just Get Up Out of Your Seat,* pages 21–32, "Just as I am?" Ask for an oral narration if desired.

Grades 4–6: Read with your older children or assign as independent reading *Team Moon,* pages 30–41. Ask for an oral or written narration if desired.

Grades 7–9: Read with your older children or assign as independent reading *Roll of Thunder, Hear My Cry,* chapter 10. Ask for an oral or written narration if desired.

Grades 10–12: Read with your older children or assign as independent reading *America: The Last Best Hope, Volume 2,* chapter 11, "The Years the Locusts Ate." Ask for an oral or written narration.

Also read together or assign as independent reading *American Voices,* pages 363–366, "Gerald R. Ford's Remarks at His Swearing-In" and selected praise songs. Ask for an oral or written narration.

Lesson 143: Geography Book and Revelation 11

Materials Needed
- *Paddle to the Sea* OR *WorldTrek*
- Outline map of United States; labeled U. S. map
- Bible
- *Come, Lord Jesus: Lessons from Revelation*
- *Discovering Doctrine* (grades 7–12)

Family Geography Book: Ask students what they recall from last time's reading about Paddle-to-the-Sea crossing two borders. Read together *Paddle to the Sea*, chapters 11–13, and ask for an oral narration OR read together *WorldTrek*, pages 185–188, and trace the Fishers' route on a map or globe.

Family Map Drill: Give each student a copy of a blank outline map of the United States and encourage them to label the states on the map. Include the optional state abbreviations challenge if desired. Compare their labeled states with a labeled United States map and make any necessary corrections. Then have them label one or two more states on their maps, copying the spelling and locations from the labeled United States map.

Family Bible Study: Complete *Come, Lord Jesus: Lessons from Revelation*, lesson 11.

Grades 10–12: Older students who are completing *Discovering Doctrine* this year should summarize their Anthropology findings this week in written form. They should also record their findings from the Revelation study under Eschatology.

Tip: Those older students who are not summarizing Discovering Doctrine *findings this term should still record doctrinal truths from* Revelation.

 # Lesson 144: *Kon Tiki*

Materials Needed
- *Stories of the Nations, Vol. 2*
- *Brother Andrew* (grades 4–6)
- *Animal Farm* (grades 7–9)
- *Stalin* (grades 10–12)

Family: Ask students what they recall about Gandhi's life. Explain that while Gandhi was working to gain independence for India, a scientist from Norway was pondering an idea. Help students find Norway on a world map or globe. Read together *Stories of the Nations, Volume 2*, chapter 26, "Kon

Heyerdahl sails Kon Tiki *raft across South Seas (1947)*

Tiki." Use your map or globe to identify the areas involved in Heyerdahl's theory and trace his route from Peru to the South Seas islands. Ask for an oral narration.

Grades 4–6: Read with your older children or assign as independent reading *Brother Andrew,* chapter 9, "Headed for an Unknown Adventure." Ask for an oral or written narration.

Grades 7–9: Read with your older children or assign as independent reading *Animal Farm,* chapter 7. Ask for an oral or written narration.

Grades 10–12: Read with your older children or assign as independent reading *Stalin,* the last half of the chapter "The Pact of Blood," approximately pages 160–173. Ask for an oral or written narration.

 # Lesson 145: The Top of the World

Materials Needed
  • *Stories of the Nations, Vol. 2*
  • *Brother Andrew* (grades 4–6)
  • *Animal Farm* (grades 7–9)
  • *Stalin* (grades 10–12)

Family: Ask students what they recall about *Kon Tiki.* Explain that today's story takes place thousands of feet above those South Seas islands, on the mountains of the Himalaya. Help students locate those mountains on the map or globe. Read together *Stories of the Nations, Volume 2,* chapter 27, "The Top of the World." Ask for an oral narration.

Hillary reaches the top of Mt. Everest (1953)

Grades 4–6: Read with your older children or assign as independent reading *Brother Andrew,* chapter 10, "An Experiment in Trusting God." Ask for an oral or written narration.

Grades 7–9: Read with your older children or assign as independent reading *Animal Farm,* chapter 8. Ask for an oral or written narration.

Grades 10–12: Read with your older children or assign as independent reading *Stalin,* the first half of the chapter "The Great Patriotic War," approximately pages 174–190. Ask for an oral or written narration.

Reminder: Get the book Mandela: The Rebel Who Led His Nation to Freedom *for Family for lesson 155.*

Lesson 146: Billy Graham, part 3

Materials Needed
  • *Billy Graham: God's Ambassador* OR *Just Get Up Out of Your Seat*

• *Team Moon* (grades 4–6)
• *Roll of Thunder, Hear My Cry* (grades 7–9)
• *America: The Last Best Hope, Vol. 2* (grades 10–12)
• *American Voices* (grades 10–12)

Family: Ask students what they recall about Billy Graham's life so far. Read together *Billy Graham: God's Ambassador*, the first half of chapter 2, "A Lifetime of Ministry Begins," approximately pages 39–55, OR *Just Get Up Out of Your Seat*, pages 33–40, "Preacher Boy." Ask for an oral narration if desired.

Grades 4–6: Read with your older children or assign as independent reading *Team Moon*, pages 42–52. Ask for an oral or written narration if desired.

Grades 7–9: Read with your older children or assign as independent reading *Roll of Thunder, Hear My Cry*, chapters 11 and 12. Ask for an oral or written narration if desired.

Grades 10–12: Read with your older children or assign as independent reading *America: The Last Best Hope, Volume 2*, the first half of chapter 12, "Reagan and Revival," approximately pages 480–507. Ask for an oral or written narration.

Also read together or assign as independent reading *American Voices*, pages 367–370, "Ronald Reagan's First Inaugural Address." Ask for an oral or written narration.

Lesson 147: Billy Graham, part 4

Materials Needed
• *Billy Graham: God's Ambassador* OR *Just Get Up Out of Your Seat*
• *Team Moon* (grades 4–6)
• *Ronald Reagan: Destiny at His Side* (grades 7–9)
• *America: The Last Best Hope, Vol. 2* (grades 10–12)
• *American Voices* (grades 10–12)

Family: Ask students what they recall from last time's reading about Rev. Graham. Read together *Billy Graham: God's Ambassador*, the last half of chapter 2, "A Lifetime of Ministry Begins," approximately pages 56–85, OR *Just Get Up Out of Your Seat*, pages 41–52, "Ask Her for a Date!" Ask for an oral narration if desired.

Grades 4–6: Read with your older children or assign as independent reading *Team Moon*, pages 53–69. Ask for an oral or written narration if desired.

Grades 7–9: Read with your older children or assign as independent reading *Ronald Reagan: Destiny at His Side*, chapters 1 and 2, "Get Us to GW!" and "Dutch." Ask for an oral or written narration.

Grades 10–12: Read with your older children or assign as independent reading *America: The Last Best Hope, Volume 2,* the last half of chapter 12, "Reagan and Revival," approximately pages 507–530. Ask for an oral or written narration.

Also read together or assign as independent reading *American Voices,* pages 371–375, "Ronald Reagan's Farewell Address." Ask for an oral or written narration.

Tip: Make sure older children are up to date with their Book of Centuries entries.

Lesson 148: Geography Book and Revelation 12

Materials Needed
- *Paddle to the Sea* OR *WorldTrek*
- Outline map of United States; labeled U. S. map
- Bible
- *Come, Lord Jesus: Lessons from Revelation*
- *Discovering Doctrine* (grades 7–12)

Family Geography Book: Ask students what they recall from last time's reading about Paddle-to-the-Sea's journey through Lake Superior. Read together *Paddle to the Sea,* chapters 14 and 15, and ask for an oral narration OR read together *WorldTrek,* pages 189–195, and trace the Fishers' route on a map or globe.

Family Map Drill: Give each student a copy of a blank outline map of the United States and encourage them to label the states on the map. Include the optional state abbreviations challenge if desired. Compare their labeled states with a labeled United States map and make any necessary corrections. Then have them label one or two more states on their maps, copying the spelling and locations from the labeled United States map.

Family Bible Study: Complete *Come, Lord Jesus: Lessons from Revelation,* lesson 12.

Grades 10–12: Older students who are completing *Discovering Doctrine* this year should summarize their Hamartiology findings this week in written form. They should also record their findings from the Revelation study under Eschatology.

Tip: Those older students who are not summarizing Discovering Doctrine *findings this term should still record doctrinal truths from* Revelation.

Lesson 149: *Sputnik*

Materials Needed
- *Stories of the Nations, Vol. 2*
- *Brother Andrew* (grades 4–6)
- *Animal Farm* (grades 7–9)
- *Stalin* (grades 10–12)

Family: Ask students what they recall about Edmund Hillary's expedition up Mount Everest. Explain that today's story involves a long-standing competition that goes way back to World War II. Read together *Stories of the Nations, Volume 2*, chapter 28, "*Sputnik*." Ask for an oral narration.

Soviet Union launches Sputnik *satellite (1957)*

Grades 4–6: Read with your older children or assign as independent reading *Brother Andrew,* chapter 11, "Behind the Iron Curtain." Ask for an oral or written narration.

Grades 7–9: Read with your older children or assign as independent reading *Animal Farm,* chapter 9. Ask for an oral or written narration.

Grades 10–12: Read with your older children or assign as independent reading *Stalin,* the last half of the chapter "The Great Patriotic War," approximately pages 190–209. Ask for an oral or written narration.

 # Lesson 150: The Berlin Wall

Materials Needed
- *Stories of the Nations, Vol. 2*
- *Brother Andrew* (grades 4–6)
- *Animal Farm* (grades 7–9)
- *Stalin* (grades 10–12)

Family: Ask students what they recall about *Sputnik*. Explain that the Soviet Union is involved in today's story as well. Read together *Stories of the Nations, Volume 2*, chapter 29, "The Berlin Wall." Use the map in the back of *Stories of the Nations, Volume 2,* to show the location of Berlin and how Europe was divided after World War II. Ask for an oral narration.

Berlin Wall divides the city of Berlin (1961–1989)

Grades 4–6: Read with your older children or assign as independent reading *Brother Andrew,* chapter 12, "The Cup of Suffering." Ask for an oral or written narration.

Grades 7–9: Read with your older children or assign as independent reading *Animal Farm,* chapter 10. Ask for an oral or written narration.

Grades 10–12: Read with your older children or assign as independent reading *Stalin,* the chapter "Into the Shadows." Ask for an oral or written narration.

Book of Centuries Timeline

President Reagan opens dialogue with Soviet Union, challenges Gorbachev to tear down the Berlin Wall (1981–1989)

 # Lesson 151: The End of the Cold War

Materials Needed
- *Stories of America, Vol. 2*
- *Our Country's Presidents*
- *Ronald Reagan: Destiny at His Side* (grades 7–9)
- *America: The Last Best Hope, Vol. 3* (grades 10–12)

Family: Ask students to reach back many years in their minds and tell what they recall about the Cold War. Read together *Stories of America, Volume 2*, chapter 33, "The End of the Cold War." Ask for an oral narration.

Look together at *Our Country's Presidents*, the section on Ronald Reagan. You will find a photograph of President Reagan and Mikhail Gorbachev. Older students may read the biographical sketch.

Grades 4–6: Help your child select one of the following presidential projects to complete over the last weeks of this term, using *Our Country's Presidents* as a reference: (1) Create a game that helps the players learn about the U. S. presidents and events that occurred during their administrations; OR (2) Make a timeline of the stories read in *Stories of America, Volume 2*, then research and write in who was U. S. president during each story's events. If desired, expand this project to include *Stories of America, Volume 1*; OR (3) Choose two U. S. presidents to read more about and prepare narrations, one oral and one written.

Grades 7–9: Read with your older children or assign as independent reading *Ronald Reagan: Destiny at His Side*, chapters 3 and 4, "Dixon" and "Lifeguard." Ask for an oral or written narration.

Grades 10–12: Read with your older children or assign as independent reading *America: The Last Best Hope, Volume 3*, the first half of chapter 1, "Enemies Abroad, Challenges at Home," approximately pages 1–24. Ask for an oral or written narration.

 # Lesson 152: Billy Graham, part 5

Materials Needed
- *Billy Graham: God's Ambassador* OR *Just Get Up Out of Your Seat*
- *Our Country's Presidents* (grades 4–6)
- *Ronald Reagan: Destiny at His Side* (grades 7–9)
- *America: The Last Best Hope, Vol. 3* (grades 10–12)

Family: Ask students what they recall about Billy Graham's life so far. Read together *Billy Graham: God's Ambassador*, chapter 3, "Millions of Lives Changed," OR *Just Get Up Out of Your Seat*, pages 53–64, "The Modesto Manifesto." Ask for an oral narration if desired.

Tip: If you are reading Billy Graham: God's Ambassador, *be sure to notice in today's chapter the photograph of Rev. Graham preaching in West Berlin and the section on his being invited to preach in the Soviet Union during the Cold War.*

Grades 4–6: Continue working on the selected presidential project, using *Our Country's Presidents* for reference as needed.

Grades 7–9: Read with your older children or assign as independent reading *Ronald Reagan: Destiny at His Side,* chapters 5 and 6, "Eureka College" and "Depression Days." Ask for an oral or written narration.

Grades 10–12: Read with your older children or assign as independent reading *America: The Last Best Hope, Volume 3,* the last half of chapter 1, "Enemies Abroad, Challenges at Home," approximately pages 24–52. Ask for an oral or written narration.

Lesson 153: Geography Book and Revelation 13

Materials Needed
- *Paddle to the Sea* OR *WorldTrek*
- Outline map of United States; labeled U. S. map
- Bible
- *Come, Lord Jesus: Lessons from Revelation*
- *Discovering Doctrine* (grades 7–12)

Family Geography Book: Ask students what they recall from last time's reading about the shipwreck and rescue. Read together *Paddle to the Sea,* chapters 16–18, and ask for an oral narration OR read together *WorldTrek,* pages 195–203, and trace the Fishers' route on a map or globe.

Family Map Drill: Give each student a copy of a blank outline map of the United States and encourage them to label the states on the map. Include the optional state abbreviations challenge if desired. Compare their labeled states with a labeled United States map and make any necessary corrections. Then have them label one or two more states on their maps, copying the spelling and locations from the labeled United States map.

Family Bible Study: Complete *Come, Lord Jesus: Lessons from Revelation,* lesson 13.

Grades 10–12: Older students who are completing *Discovering Doctrine* this year should summarize their Soteriology findings this week in written form. They should also record their findings from the Revelation study under Eschatology.

Tip: Those older students who are not summarizing Discovering Doctrine *findings this term should still record doctrinal truths from Revelation.*

Book of Centuries
Timeline

Volcano forms Paricutin in Mexico
(1943–1952)

Volcano forms island of Surtsey
(1963)

 # Lesson 154: New Lands

Materials Needed
- *Stories of the Nations, Vol. 2*
- *Brother Andrew* (grades 4–6)
- *Rescue and Redeem* (grades 7–12)

Family: Ask students if they have heard of any new lands that have appeared on Earth during the last century. Read together *Stories of the Nations, Volume 2*, chapter 30, "New Lands." Ask for an oral narration.

Grades 4–6: Read with your older children or assign as independent reading *Brother Andrew*, chapter 13, "Don't Take No for an Answer." Ask for an oral or written narration.

Grades 7–12: Read with your older children or assign as independent reading *Rescue and Redeem*, pages 193–198, "Big Moments in Modern Christianity." Ask for an oral or written narration.

Reminder: Get the book Swifter, Higher, Stronger: A Photographic History of the Summer Olympics *for grades 7–9 for lesson 164.*

 # Lesson 155: Nelson Mandela, part 1

Materials Needed
- *Mandela: The Rebel Who Led His Nation to Freedom*
- *Brother Andrew* (grades 4–6)
- *Rescue and Redeem* (grades 7–12)

Nelson Mandela leads fight against
apartheid in South Africa, becomes
president (1948–1999)

Family: Write the word "apartheid" on a small whiteboard or sheet of paper. Show the word to the students and ask if they know what it means. Explain that the word means "apartness," and was a rule of life between white men and black men in South Africa for many years. The man you will read about next helped change that rule. Read together *Mandela*, pages 6–15, from "Childhood on the Veldt" to "Starting School." Ask for an oral narration.

Grades 4–6: Read with your older children or assign as independent reading *Brother Andrew*, chapter 14, "Someone to Share His Life With." Ask for an oral or written narration.

Grades 7–12: Read with your older children or assign as independent reading *Rescue and Redeem*, pages 199–216, "C. S. Lewis." Ask for an oral or written narration.

 # Lesson 156: September 11, 2001

Materials Needed
- *Stories of America, Vol. 2*

- *Our Country's Presidents*
- *Ronald Reagan: Destiny at His Side* (grades 7–9)
- *America: The Last Best Hope, Vol. 3* (grades 10–12)

Family: Read together *Stories of America, Volume 2,* chapter 34, "September 11, 2001." Ask for an oral narration. Look together at *Our Country's Presidents,* the section on George W. Bush. Notice especially the photograph of President Bush at Ground Zero. Older students may read the biographical sketch.

Grades 4–6: Continue working on the selected presidential project, using *Our Country's Presidents* for reference as needed.

Grades 7–9: Read with your older children or assign as independent reading *Ronald Reagan: Destiny at His Side,* chapters 7 and 8, "On the Radio" and "A Household Name." Ask for an oral or written narration.

Grades 10–12: Read with your older children or assign as independent reading *America: The Last Best Hope, Volume 3,* the first half of chapter 2, "Rise of the Boomer," approximately pages 53–85. Ask for an oral or written narration.

 Lesson 157: Billy Graham, part 6

Materials Needed
- *Billy Graham: God's Ambassador* OR *Just Get Up Out of Your Seat*
- *Our Country's Presidents* (grades 4–6)
- *Ronald Reagan: Destiny at His Side* (grades 7–9)
- *America: The Last Best Hope, Vol. 3* (grades 10–12)

Family: Ask students what they recall from last time's reading about Billy Graham. Read together *Billy Graham: God's Ambassador,* chapter 4, "Reaching Out to a Broken World," OR *Just Get Up Out of Your Seat,* pages 65–80, "Puff Graham!" Ask for an oral narration if desired.

Tip: If you are reading Billy Graham: God's Ambassador, *notice especially the photographs of Rev. Graham with Rev. King, Graham's visits to Korea and Vietnam, and his meeting with a worker at Ground Zero.*

Grades 4–6: Continue working on the selected presidential project, using *Our Country's Presidents* for reference as needed.

Grades 7–9: Read with your older children or assign as independent reading *Ronald Reagan: Destiny at His Side,* chapters 9 and 10, "Hollywood" and "All American." Ask for an oral or written narration.

Grades 10–12: Read with your older children or assign as independent reading *America: The Last Best Hope, Volume 3,* the last half of chapter 2,

Book of Centuries Timeline

Terrorist attack on U. S. World Trade Center towers and Pentagon (2001)

"Rise of the Boomer," approximately pages 85–116. Ask for an oral or written narration.

Tip: Make sure older children are up to date with their Book of Centuries entries.

 Lesson 158: Geography Book and Revelation 14

Materials Needed
- *Paddle to the Sea* OR *WorldTrek*
- Outline map of United States; labeled U. S. map
- Bible
- *Come, Lord Jesus: Lessons from Revelation*
- *Discovering Doctrine* (grades 7–12)

Family Geography Book: Ask students what they recall from last time's reading about Paddle-to-the-Sea's time on Lake Michigan. Read together *Paddle to the Sea*, chapters 19 and 20, and ask for an oral narration OR read together *WorldTrek*, pages 203–211, and trace the Fishers' route on a map or globe.

Family Map Drill: Give each student a copy of a blank outline map of the United States and encourage them to label the states on the map. Include the optional state abbreviations challenge if desired. Compare their labeled states with a labeled United States map and make any necessary corrections. Then have them label one or two more states on their maps, copying the spelling and locations from the labeled United States map.

Family Bible Study: Complete *Come, Lord Jesus: Lessons from Revelation*, lesson 14.

Grades 10–12: Older students who are completing *Discovering Doctrine* this year should summarize their Angelology findings this week in written form. They should also record their findings from the Revelation study under Eschatology.

Tip: Those older students who are not summarizing Discovering Doctrine *findings this term should still record doctrinal truths from* Revelation.

 Lesson 159: Nelson Mandela, part 2

Materials Needed
- *Mandela: The Rebel Who Led His Nation to Freedom*

• *Brother Andrew* (grades 4–6)
• *Rescue and Redeem* (grades 7–12)

Family: Ask students what they recall from last time's reading about Nelson Mandela's childhood. Read together *Mandela*, pages 16–25, from "Leaving Qunu" to "European Domination." Ask for an oral narration.

Grades 4–6: Read with your older children or assign as independent reading *Brother Andrew,* chapter 15, "Nerves of Steel." Ask for an oral or written narration.

Grades 7–12: Read with your older children or assign as independent reading *Rescue and Redeem*, pages 217–234, "Janani Luwum." Ask for an oral or written narration.

 # Lesson 160: Nelson Mandela, part 3

Materials Needed
• *Mandela: The Rebel Who Led His Nation to Freedom*
• *Brother Andrew* (grades 4–6)
• *Rescue and Redeem* (grades 7–12)

Family: Ask students what they recall from last time's reading about Nelson Mandela's life in the Great Place and the history of South Africa. Read together *Mandela*, pages 26–35, from "Becoming a Man" to "Johannesburg." Ask for an oral narration.

Grades 4–6: Read with your older children or assign as independent reading *Brother Andrew,* chapter 16, "Into the Soviet Union." Ask for an oral or written narration.

Grades 7–12: Read with your older children or assign as independent reading *Rescue and Redeem*, pages 235–244, "Other Modern Christians" and "The Future Lives."

 # Lesson 161: A New Kind of War

Materials Needed
• *Stories of America, Vol. 2*
• *Our Country's Presidents* (grades 4–6)
• *Ronald Reagan: Destiny at His Side* (grades 7–9)
• *America: The Last Best Hope, Vol. 3* (grades 10–12)

Family: Ask students what they recall about September 11, 2001. Read together *Stories of America, Volume 2,* chapter 35, "A New Kind of War." Ask for an oral narration.

Grades 4–6: Continue working on the selected presidential project, using *Our Country's Presidents* for reference as needed.

Grades 7–9: Read with your older children or assign as independent reading *Ronald Reagan: Destiny at His Side,* chapters 11 and 12, "Fort Roach" and "SAG." Ask for an oral or written narration.

Grades 10–12: Read with your older children or assign as independent reading *America: The Last Best Hope, Volume 3,* chapter 3, "Into the Fire." Ask for an oral or written narration.

 # Lesson 162: Billy Graham, part 7

Materials Needed
- *Billy Graham: God's Ambassador* OR *Just Get Up Out of Your Seat*
- *Our Country's Presidents* (grades 4–6)
- *Ronald Reagan: Destiny at His Side* (grades 7–9)
- *America: The Last Best Hope, Vol. 3* (grades 10–12)
- *American Voices* (grades 10–12)

Family: Ask students what they recall from last time's reading about Billy Graham. Read together *Billy Graham: God's Ambassador,* the first half of chapter 5, "Inspiring Others," approximately pages 139–151, OR *Just Get Up Out of Your Seat,* pages 81–92, "A Brush with History." Ask for an oral narration if desired.

Tip: If you are reading Billy Graham: God's Ambassador, *you will have a prime opportunity to review many modern U. S. presidents as you go through chapter 5. Encourage students to make personal connections by recalling the events they have read about that are connected with each president as they look through the photographs.*

Grades 4–6: Continue working on the selected presidential project, using *Our Country's Presidents* for reference as needed.

Grades 7–9: Read with your older children or assign as independent reading *Ronald Reagan: Destiny at His Side,* chapters 13 and 14, "Nancy" and "Electric Living." Ask for an oral or written narration.

Grades 10–12: Read with your older children or assign as independent reading *America: The Last Best Hope, Volume 3,* the first half of chapter 4, "Bush and the Age of Terror," approximately pages 153–182. Ask for an oral or written narration.

Also read together or assign as independent reading *American Voices,* pages 386–392, President Bush's "National Day of Prayer and Remembrance Speech" and "Address To a Joint Session of Congress and the American People." Ask for an oral or written narration.

Lesson 163: Geography Book and Revelation 15

Materials Needed
- *Paddle to the Sea* OR *WorldTrek*
- Outline map of United States; labeled U. S. map
- Bible
- *Come, Lord Jesus: Lessons from Revelation*
- *Discovering Doctrine* (grades 7–12)

Family Geography Book: Ask students what they recall from last time's reading about Paddle-to-the-Sea in Lake Huron. Read together *Paddle to the Sea*, chapters 21–23, and ask for an oral narration OR read together *WorldTrek*, pages 212–217, and trace the Fishers' route on a map or globe.

Family Map Drill: Give each student a copy of a blank outline map of the United States and encourage them to label the states on the map. Include the optional state abbreviations challenge if desired. Compare their labeled states with a labeled United States map and make any necessary corrections. Then have them label one or two more states on their maps, copying the spelling and locations from the labeled United States map.

Family Bible Study: Complete *Come, Lord Jesus: Lessons from Revelation*, lesson 15.

Grades 10–12: Older students who are completing *Discovering Doctrine* this year should summarize their Ecclesiology findings this week in written form. They should also record their findings from the Revelation study under Eschatology.

Tip: Those older students who are not summarizing Discovering Doctrine *findings this term should still record doctrinal truths from* Revelation.

Lesson 164: Nelson Mandela, part 4

Materials Needed
- *Mandela: The Rebel Who Led His Nation to Freedom*
- *Brother Andrew* (grades 4–6)
- *Swifter, Higher, Stronger* (grades 7–9)
- *How Should We Then Live?* OR *7 Men Who Rule the World from the Grave* (grades 10–12)

Family: Ask students what they recall from last time's reading about Nelson Mandela's school years. Read together *Mandela*, pages 36–43, from "Politics and Marriage" to "On the Run." Ask for an oral narration.

Grades 4–6: Read with your older children or assign as independent reading *Brother Andrew,* chapter 17, "The Bamboo Curtain." Ask for an oral or written narration.

Grades 7–9: Read with your older children or assign as independent reading *Swifter, Higher, Stronger,* chapter 1, "The Games Reborn." Ask for an oral or written narration.

Grades 10–12: Read with your older children or assign as independent reading *How Should We Then Live?,* chapter 8, "The Breakdown in Philosophy and Science," OR *7 Men Who Rule the World from the Grave,* chapter 7, "The Coming of the Strange Fire." Ask for an oral or written narration.

Lesson 165: Nelson Mandela, part 5

Materials Needed
- *Mandela: The Rebel Who Led His Nation to Freedom*
- *Brother Andrew* (grades 4–6)
- *Swifter, Higher, Stronger* (grades 7–9)
- *How Should We Then Live?* OR *7 Men Who Rule the World from the Grave* (grades 10–12)

Family: Ask students what they recall from last time's reading about Nelson Mandela's struggle against apartheid. Read together *Mandela,* pages 44–51, from "Life Imprisonment" to "Free Mandela!" Ask for an oral narration.

Grades 4–6: Read with your older children or assign as independent reading *Brother Andrew,* chapter 18, "The Fight Continues." Ask for an oral or written narration.

Grades 7–9: Read with your older children or assign as independent reading *Swifter, Higher, Stronger,* chapter 2, "Women Dig in Their Heels." Ask for an oral or written narration.

Grades 10–12: Read with your older children or assign as independent reading *How Should We Then Live?,* chapter 9, "Modern Philosophy and Modern Theology," OR *7 Men Who Rule the World from the Grave,* chapter 8, "Looking Within: Sigmund Freud." Ask for an oral or written narration.

 # Lesson 166: The Information Age

Materials Needed
- *Stories of America, Vol. 2*
- *Our Country's Presidents* (grades 4–6)
- *Ronald Reagan: Destiny at His Side* (grades 7–9)
- *America: The Last Best Hope, Vol. 3* (grades 10–12)

Family: Read together *Stories of America, Volume 2,* chapter 36, "The Information Age and a Farewell." Ask for an oral narration.

Grades 4–6: Continue working on the selected presidential project, using *Our Country's Presidents* for reference as needed.

Grades 7–9: Read with your older children or assign as independent reading *Ronald Reagan: Destiny at His Side,* chapters 15 and 16, "Governor" and "The Will of the People." Ask for an oral or written narration.

Grades 10–12: Read with your older children or assign as independent reading *America: The Last Best Hope, Volume 3,* the last half of chapter 4, "Bush and the Age of Terror," approximately pages 182–201. Ask for an oral or written narration.

 # Lesson 167: Billy Graham, part 8

Materials Needed
- *Billy Graham: God's Ambassador* OR *Just Get Up Out of Your Seat*
- *Our Country's Presidents* (grades 4–6)
- *Ronald Reagan: Destiny at His Side* (grades 7–9)
- *America: The Last Best Hope, Vol. 3* (grades 10–12)

Family: Ask students what they recall from last time's reading about Billy Graham. Read together *Billy Graham: God's Ambassador,* the last half of chapter 5, "Inspiring Others," approximately pages 152–177, OR *Just Get Up Out of Your Seat,* pages 93–104, "A Different Europe." Ask for an oral narration if desired.

Grades 4–6: Continue working on the selected presidential project, using *Our Country's Presidents* for reference as needed.

Grades 7–9: Read with your older children or assign as independent reading *Ronald Reagan: Destiny at His Side,* chapters 17 and 18, "A Survivor" and "Meeting the Challenge." Ask for an oral or written narration.

Grades 10–12: Read with your older children or assign as independent reading *America: The Last Best Hope, Volume 3,* chapter 5, "In War and Culture." Ask for an oral or written narration.

Tip: Make sure older children are up to date with their Book of Centuries entries.

 # Lesson 168: Geography Book and Revelation 16

Materials Needed
- *Paddle to the Sea* OR *WorldTrek*
- Outline map of United States; labeled U. S. map

• Bible
• *Come, Lord Jesus: Lessons from Revelation*
• *Discovering Doctrine* (grades 7–12)

Family Geography Book: Ask students what they recall from last time's reading about Paddle-to-the-Sea's trip to Lake Erie and Lake Ontario. Read together *Paddle to the Sea*, chapters 24 and 25, and ask for an oral narration OR read together *WorldTrek*, pages 217–223, and trace the Fishers' route on a map or globe.

Family Map Drill: Give each student a copy of a blank outline map of the United States and encourage them to label the states on the map. Include the optional state abbreviations challenge if desired. Compare their labeled states with a labeled United States map and make any necessary corrections. Then have them label one or two more states on their maps, copying the spelling and locations from the labeled United States map.

Family Bible Study: Complete *Come, Lord Jesus: Lessons from Revelation*, lesson 16.

Grades 10–12: Older students who are completing *Discovering Doctrine* may use this week as a catch-up week for writing their doctrinal summaries. They should also record their findings from the Revelation study under Eschatology.

Tip: Those older students who are not summarizing Discovering Doctrine *findings this term should still record doctrinal truths from* Revelation.

 # Lesson 169: Nelson Mandela, part 6

Materials Needed
• *Mandela: The Rebel Who Led His Nation to Freedom*
• *Swifter, Higher, Stronger* (grades 7–9)
• *How Should We Then Live?* OR *7 Men Who Rule the World from the Grave* (grades 10–12)

Family: Ask students what they recall from last time's reading about Nelson Mandela's imprisonment. Read together *Mandela*, pages 52–59, from "Release from Prison" to "Retirement." Ask for an oral narration.

Grades 7–9: Read with your older children or assign as independent reading *Swifter, Higher, Stronger*, chapter 3, "Breakthrough Athletes." Ask for an oral or written narration.

Tip: One of the athletes mentioned is Greg Louganis, who later announced that he was a homosexual. It is simply stated as fact with no interpretive commentary.

Grades 10–12: Read with your older children or assign as independent reading *How Should We Then Live?*, chapter 10, "Modern Art, Music, Literature, and Films," OR *7 Men Who Rule the World from the Grave*, chapter 9, "The Vast Emergence: John Dewey." Ask for an oral or written narration.

 # Lesson 170: Old Thrones

Materials Needed
- *Stories of the Nations, Vol. 2*
- *Swifter, Higher, Stronger* (grades 7–9)
- *How Should We Then Live?* OR *7 Men Who Rule the World from the Grave* (grades 10–12)

Family: Read together *Stories of the Nations, Volume 2*, chapter 31, "Old Thrones." Ask for an oral narration.

Grades 7–9: Read with your older children or assign as independent reading *Swifter, Higher, Stronger*, chapter 4, "Controversies Cast a Shadow." Ask for an oral or written narration.

Tip: The controversies covered in this chapter include amateurism, gender testing, drug testing (mentioning some results of steroid use), and politics.

Grades 10–12: Read with your older children or assign as independent reading *How Should We Then Live?*, chapter 11, "Our Society," OR *7 Men Who Rule the World from the Grave*, chapter 10, "New Hope for the Nations: John Maynard Keynes." Ask for an oral or written narration.

 # Lesson 171: Billy Graham, part 9

Materials Needed
- *Billy Graham: God's Ambassador* OR *Just Get Up Out of Your Seat*
- *Our Country's Presidents* (grades 4–6)
- *Ronald Reagan: Destiny at His Side* (grades 7–9)
- *America: The Last Best Hope, Vol. 3* (grades 10–12)

Family: Read together *Billy Graham: God's Ambassador*, chapter 6, "Reflections from Home," and pages 193–206, OR *Just Get Up Out of Your Seat*, pages 105–116, "105 Degrees in the Shade." Ask for an oral narration if desired.

Tip: If your family has participated in Operation Christmas Child, help your children make that personal connection when you read about Samaritan's Purse, the sponsoring organization of that project.

---

*Book of Centuries
Timeline*

Grades 4–6: Finish working on the selected presidential project, using *Our Country's Presidents* for reference as needed. Projects will be presented in lesson 172.

Grades 7–9: Read with your older children or assign as independent reading *Ronald Reagan: Destiny at His Side,* chapters 19 and 20, "Taking Action" and "Destiny at His Side." Ask for an oral or written narration.

Grades 10–12: Read with your older children or assign as independent reading *America: The Last Best Hope, Volume 3,* the first half of chapter 6, "Peril and Promise," approximately pages 229–256. Ask for an oral or written narration.

Lesson 172: America

Materials Needed
- *Stories of America, Vol. 2*
- *Just Get Up Out of Your Seat* (if needed)
- *America: The Last Best Hope, Vol. 3* (grades 10–12)

Family: Read together the poem "America" on page 225 of *Stories of America, Volume 2.* Spend some time in prayer for our nation.

    If you have been reading *Just Get Up Out of Your Seat,* read pages 117–131, "Moscow Tourist" and "Global Relief," to finish the book today. Ask for an oral narration if desired.

Grades 4–6: Ask your child to present his selected presidential project to the family.

Grades 10–12: Read with your older children or assign as independent reading *America: The Last Best Hope, Volume 3,* the last half of chapter 6, "Peril and Promise," approximately pages 256–270. Ask for an oral or written narration.

Lesson 173: Geography Book and Revelation 17

Materials Needed
- *Paddle to the Sea* OR *WorldTrek*
- Outline map of United States; labeled U. S. map
- Bible
- *Come, Lord Jesus: Lessons from Revelation*
- *Discovering Doctrine* (grades 7–12)

Family Geography Book: Ask students what they recall from last time's reading about Paddle-to-the-Sea and the St. Lawrence River. Read together *Paddle to the Sea*, chapters 26 and 27, and ask for an oral narration OR read together *WorldTrek*, pages 224–228, and trace the Fishers' route on a map or globe.

Family Map Drill: Give each student a copy of a blank outline map of the United States and encourage them to label the states on the map. Include the optional state abbreviations challenge if desired. Compare their labeled states with a labeled United States map and make any necessary corrections. Then have them label one or two more states on their maps, copying the spelling and locations from the labeled United States map.

Family Bible Study: Complete *Come, Lord Jesus: Lessons from Revelation*, lesson 17.

Grades 10–12: Older students who are completing *Discovering Doctrine* this year should record their findings from the Revelation study under Eschatology, then summarize their Eschatology findings this week in written form.

Tip: Those older students who are not summarizing Discovering Doctrine *findings this term should still record doctrinal truths from* Revelation.

 # Lesson 174: The Channel Tunnel

Materials Needed
- *Stories of the Nations, Vol. 2*
- *Swifter, Higher, Stronger* (grades 7–9)
- *How Should We Then Live?* OR *7 Men Who Rule the World from the Grave* (grades 10–12)

Family: Ask students what they recall about the oldest monarchy in the world and about the throne of England. Read together *Stories of the Nations, Volume 2*, chapter 32, "The Channel Tunnel." Ask for an oral narration.

Grades 7–9: Read with your older children or assign as independent reading *Swifter, Higher, Stronger,* chapter 5, "Unlikely Heroes." Ask for an oral or written narration.

Grades 10–12: Read with your older children or assign as independent reading *How Should We Then Live?*, chapter 12, "Manipulation and the New Elite," OR *7 Men Who Rule the World from the Grave*, chapter 11, "The Advent of Diffusion: Soren Kierkegaard." Ask for an oral or written narration.

Tunnel open under English Channel to connect France and England (1994)

Lesson 175: Catch Up

Materials Needed
- *How Should We Then Live?* OR *7 Men Who Rule the World from the Grave* (grades 10–12)

Family: Use today to catch up on any world history reading assigned.

Grades 10–12: Read with your older children or assign as independent reading *How Should We Then Live?,* chapter 13, "The Alternatives," OR *7 Men Who Rule the World from the Grave,* chapter 12, "Who Shall Overcome?" Ask for an oral or written narration.

 Lesson 176: American History Project or Exam

Materials Needed
- *America: The Last Best Hope, Vol. 3* (grades 10–12)

Family: Do a hands-on project (see below), or use the questions below to begin the students' exam on American history.

Grades 1–3: Tell the story of Martin Luther King, Jr.
Grades 4–6: Tell the story of the Civil Rights movement, including Rev. Martin Luther King, Jr.'s role in it.
Grades 7–9: Tell in full about the Cold War: how it began, who was involved, how it ended, and some of the contests during its existence.
Grades 10–12: Compare and contrast the Cold War and the War on Terrorism. Be sure to include the participants, the strategies, the contests, the challenges, and the effects on the American people.

Optional Hands-On Project: Select a hands-on project from the Links and Tips page: http://simplycharlottemason.com/books/modern/links-tip/

Grades 10–12: Read with your older children or assign as independent reading *America: The Last Best Hope, Volume 3,* Epilogue.

 Lesson 177: American History Project or Exam

Family: Finish your selected hands-on project, or use the questions below to continue the students' exam on American history.

Grades 1–3: Tell the story of another hero in modern America about whom you read this term.

Grades 4–6: Tell all you know about how man walked on the moon.

Grades 7–9: "Let's roll!": Tell in full who said that phrase, when, in what situation, what happened, and how that event affects life in America today.

Grades 10–12: Based on your reading, who would you consider to be the greatest American president? Explain your answer in full, giving reasons and evidence from American history to support your opinion.

Lesson 178: Geography and Bible Exams

Family Geography Exam: Use the questions below according to the book you have been reading.

Paddle to the Sea: Show on a map where Paddle-to-the-Sea traveled, labeling the lakes as you go.

WorldTrek: Select two of the countries the Fishers have visited in the book and tell all you remember about each: India, Thailand, China, Japan, Australia, Rarotonga.

Map Drill: Give each student a copy of a blank outline map of the United States and ask them to label as many of the states as they can. Include the optional abbreviations challenge if desired.

Bible Exam: If someone asked you what the book of Revelation is about, how would you explain it? *For older children:* Name at least three common themes you see woven throughout the book.

Discovering Doctrine: Those students who summarized their findings and wrote personal doctrinal statements should turn them in for final review.

Lesson 179: World History Exam

Family: Use the questions below to begin the students' exam on Modern world history.

Grades 1–3: Tell a story of an accomplishment and the person who accomplished it about which you read this term.

Grades 4–6: Explain what the Iron Curtain was and tell what life was like for Christians who lived behind it.

Grades 7–9: Tell the story of *Animal Farm* and explain the lessons about government that it holds.

Grades 10–12: Compare and contrast Hitler and Stalin: the ways they came to power, their styles of governing, their personalities, and how their ideas affected the people of their countries.

TERM

Book of Centuries
Timeline

 # Lesson 180: World History Exam

Family: Use the questions below to continue the students' exam on Modern world history.

Grades 1–3: Tell a story of someone or something that traveled about which you read this term.

Grades 4–6: Tell about a person whose story you read this term who led his nation toward change.

Grades 7–9: Select three of the following and tell those stories in full: the creation of Israel, the discovery of the Dead Sea scrolls, Gandhi, *Kon Tiki*, climbing Mount Everest, *Sputnik*, Nelson Mandela, the Channel Tunnel.

Grades 10–12: Compare and contrast Gandhi and Nelson Mandela: their backgrounds, their countries' situations, their ways of protesting, and their lives after they became well-known.

United States Abbreviations List

AL _____	MT _____
AK _____	NE _____
AZ _____	NV _____
AR _____	NH _____
CA _____	NJ _____
CO _____	NM _____
CT _____	NY _____
DE _____	NC _____
FL _____	ND _____
GA _____	OH _____
HI _____	OK _____
ID _____	OR _____
IL _____	PA _____
IN _____	RI _____
IA _____	SC _____
KS _____	SD _____
KY _____	TN _____
LA _____	TX _____
ME _____	UT _____
MD _____	VT _____
MA _____	VA _____
MI _____	WA _____
MN _____	WV _____
MS _____	WI _____
MO _____	WY _____